Playful Little Knits

costumes and clothes for a simple sewn doll

Rachel Manring

DEDICATION

To my mother, Nancy Manring, who taught me to knit and sew

ACKNOWLEDGMENTS

I owe my family untold gratitude for their patience, understanding, and good humor. I love you all more than I can say.

Thanks to Richard Machalek and family for the use of their doll furniture (pages 66 and 70), designed and built by Henrietta Machalek of Temple, Texas, circa 1970.

Martingale & Company
19021 120th Ave. NE, Suite 102
Bothell, WA 98011-9511 USA
www.martingale-pub.com

Printed in China
16 15 14 13 12 11 8 7 6 5 4 3 2 1

Library of Congress Cataloging-in-Publication Data is available upon request.

ISBN: 978-1-60468-038-6

Credits

President & CEO – Tom Wierzbicki
Editor in Chief – Mary V. Green
Managing Editor – Tina Cook
Developmental Editor – Karen Costello Soltys
Technical Editor – Ursula Reikes
Copy Editor – Sheila Chapman Ryan
Design Director – Stan Green
Production Manager – Regina Girard
Illustrator – Robin Strobel
Cover & Text Designer – Shelly Garrison
Photographer – Brent Kane

Mission Statement

Dedicated to providing quality products and service to inspire creativity.

Contents

Introduction

When I was eight years old, my best friend, Melissa, and I spent many hours on her bedroom floor playing with Barbie dolls. Melissa had a Barbie car, airplane, townhouse, and a whole dresser drawer full of Barbie clothes. Her aunt, whom I never met, knit many of the Barbie clothes. They were all in the same style—only the colors varied. I remember wondering why a grown-up would spend her time making so many Barbie clothes. No adult I knew played with dolls.

Decades later, I have some understanding of a knitter's obsession. I still don't know any adults who admit to playing with dolls, but I know lots of them who love to knit, as I do myself. Knitting is addictively fun, like childhood playtime. To me, making toys also feels like playing. If I lived in a different time, I would be the village toymaker. Makers of toys have at least as much fun making the toys as children do playing with them. I think this is particularly true of making dolls and their clothes.

I've named my doll Baby Whimsy. The body is sewn from plain, inexpensive, easy-to-use fabric, and the outfits are all knitted. Any intermediate knitter who can knit a basic sweater, sock, or mitten can knit Baby Whimsy's wardrobe. The garments are mostly knit in the round in stockinette stitch, and can be made with small amounts of scrap yarn. Most of the garments have instructions for various knitting gauges, so the knitter can make them using whatever yarn is on hand.

Baby Whimsy is about the same size as a Beanie Baby toy. You don't have to be an accomplished seamstress to sew the baby doll. You do need a sewing machine and basic sewing skills, or the willingness to acquire them. The doll is made using a straight stitch on the sewing machine and some hand stitching. Don't assume that if you've never sewn anything you can't make Baby Whimsy. The instructions and illustrations are clear. (And there are no zippers!)

One of the pleasures of knitting—or any form of crafting—is the acquisition of new skills. We can all do more than we think we can. The more skills we have, the more creative possibilities are open to us. Our powers increase. It's very satisfying to gain a new ability, or to put together various skills to do something new. Making Baby Whimsy and her wardrobe offers you the opportunity to do this. Think how proud you'll feel when you make a new toy on your own.

However, if it does happen that you can't overcome your sewing phobia or your sewing machine is rusty, missing parts, or entirely absent, find a friend to sew the doll for you while you knit for her. A quilter can make this doll, and we all know at least one of them. Your friend could make two dolls, and you can make the dolls' clothes. Then you and your friend will have matching toys. You may feel like you're eight years old again!

Inspiration

whim•sy (hwim´zee, wim´zee), *noun., pl.* **-sies**. a quaint or fanciful quality

Where does inspiration come from? This is a big question with a different answer from everyone who has ever been inspired. For me, it comes in fleeting ideas that sometimes arrive from nowhere in particular, but are often sparked by something tangible. A word that comes to mind when I consider how my ideas begin is whim. That's where Baby Whimsy got her name. Inspiration was a scrap of yarn my mother gave me that was too small to make anything out of, or so I first thought. It was black eyelash yarn, not something I would usually knit with. But I looked at it, handled it, and thought, "What can I do with this?" Doll hair was the first thought that came to me, for a small doll. I followed this whim until I had a doll with her very own zoological wardrobe. Maybe this little doll will encourage you to follow some of your own whims.

Materials—Use What You Have

One of the pleasures of crafting is that sometimes we have the power to create something from nothing, or next to nothing. This was the case for me when I made my first Baby Whimsy doll. I used an old peach-colored cotton shirt for the body of the doll and I fiddled with a scrap of yarn until it turned into a little wig. I had embroidery thread and polyester stuffing in my supplies, and soon I had created a doll without spending any money. As a knitter, of course, I have a stash of yarn that includes lots of small bits. These eventually became the doll's clothes. My designs were largely influenced by what I already possessed. This can be the case for anyone who makes the projects in this book. They are ideal projects to use up leftovers from other projects.

Some of the supplies used to make Baby Whimsy and her wardrobe

I envision a growing population of little dolls lovingly made from materials that might have otherwise been overlooked, discarded, or left indefinitely in the dark recesses of a crowded yarn stash. This is a special kind of recycling or scavenging. Creativity is stimulated by limitations. Challenge yourself to see how many of these projects you can complete with supplies you already have.

BODIES

The dolls can be made from any medium-weight woven fabric: quilter's cotton, muslin, flannel, etc. Or recycle an old cotton shirt to make four or five dolls.

Use any shade of fabric you desire for the baby's skin.

GARMENTS

The garments are made from a wide variety of yarns in different weights. None of the projects require more than one ball of yarn, and most of them use significantly less than one ball, especially if you use fingering-weight yarn. The shirt and pants require such small amounts of yarn that they can be made from leftovers from a pair of socks.

The Basic Baby Suit instructions are given in three weights of yarn: fingering, sport, and DK. This garment is the basis for the animal costumes. So, for example, the body of the lion costume is knit from fingering weight, but you can use sport- or DK-weight yarn. In each of the patterns, you'll follow the Basic Baby Suit instructions for whatever weight yarn you are using for the body of the costume. There are additional instructions for the details of the animal costumes. Parentheses are used to separate the instructions for the various yarn weights with fingering first, sport second, and DK third, like this: fingering (sport, DK).

HAIR

The doll's hair is made from novelty yarn. Eyelash yarn works particularly well, but some other types of fuzzy yarn will also work. A yarn that I particularly like is Splash from Crystal Palace Yarns. It's very soft and knits into a thick wig. Another suitable yarn that's widely available and inexpensive is Fun Fur by Lion Brand

Yarn. It comes in various shades that are great for hair. Additional yarns used in this book are Allure from Patons, Boa from Bernat, and Fizz from Crystal Palace Yarns.

The doll's wig requires between 6 and 12 yards of yarn, so one ball can be used for several dolls or shared with your doll-making friends. If you use Fun Fur or another yarn that has a longer "lash," once you have the wig on the doll, you can trim the hair shorter if you like.

FACES

The features of the dolls in this book are stitched with embroidery thread. Alternatively, they can be painted on with fabric paint or drawn with fabric markers. You could try beads or buttons for the eyes. Seed beads are the perfect size for little earrings. Just be careful not to give a toy with buttons or beads on it to a very small child because of the choking hazard posed if the beads or buttons are pulled off and put in the mouth.

BUTTONS AND NOSES

The small buttons used in these projects can be purchased or recycled from a worn-out garment. I like to make buttons from polymer clay because I can customize the color to match the outfit (See "Make Your Own Buttons" on page 8). Noses for the clown and pig are also made from polymer clay. Instructions for making noses are included with the projects.

These yarns for the doll's hair (shown actual size) came from my own stash and some are not identifiable because they lost their label. The purpose of the photograph is to give you something to compare your own yarn with. If you have a yarn that looks similar to one of the yarns in the picture, it will likely work for Baby Whimsy's hair.

Make Your Own Buttons

Polymer clay is a versatile clay-like plastic that can be easily formed into shapes and baked in a home oven to harden it. There are a few different brands available at craft stores. It comes packaged in small amounts and in an array of colors. Artists use it to make complex and beautiful sculptures, but I use it to make simple buttons.

Buttons made from polymer clay

I'm no sculptor, but I can play with clay, mix it into the exact shade I need, and shape it into buttons. (I can also delegate this task to my children, who adamantly refuse to knit.) It takes very little clay to make buttons. Long ago I bought a few bricks of basic colors of whatever polymer clay was on sale at the time, and these have lasted me years. It's very convenient to have the raw materials on hand whenever I need some custom buttons.

Begin by conditioning the clay. This means softening the clay so it's easier to form. The clay can be warmed slightly by putting it in your pocket for a while. Then play with it—squish it around, form and reform it into snakes and balls—until it's smooth and workable. You will need very small amounts of clay for the buttons so the conditioning part doesn't take long.

Next, mix the clay colors until you have the color you want. I usually start with a piece of white clay and add colors to it. Of course, you can just use the colors that the clay comes in, but it's not hard to mix your own custom shade and this is one of the advantages of making your own buttons in the first place. I often mix two colors or shades incompletely, resulting in a marbled or flecked finished piece.

To form the buttons, roll the clay into pea-sized balls, one for each button. Flatten the balls to make the buttons, trying to make them all as close to the same size as possible. Use a tapestry needle to make two holes in the center of each button for sewing the button in place. Turn the button over and make sure the holes are large enough on each side of the button. Bake the buttons according to the instructions on the packaging. The finished buttons are washable.

There are tools that are helpful in working with clay, like special rolling pins and blades for cutting, but they're not necessary if you're just making simple buttons. If you find that you like working with polymer clay and want to learn more, get some books about it. It's a fascinating product with many uses.

NEEDLES AND HOOKS

The garments are all knit, but a crochet hook is handy for picking up stitches and making the hairpieces.

Knitting Needles

I prefer to use short, double-pointed needles for these small garments. The most comfortable length for me are 5"-long wooden needles, though 6"-long needles also work just fine. The 5" length fits well into my hand and is large enough to hold the projects' stitches. Wood holds onto the stitches better than aluminum or plastic. There are two brands of 5"-long double-pointed needles that I particularly like. One is Knit Picks Harmony needles, made from laminated birch wood with very pointed tips. The other is Brittany, also made of birch wood and with more blunted tips than the Knit Picks needles. The 5" Knit Picks needles are only available in small diameters, the largest one being size 3 (3.5 mm). Brittany 5" needles are available in sizes 0 (2.0 mm) through 10 (6.0 mm).

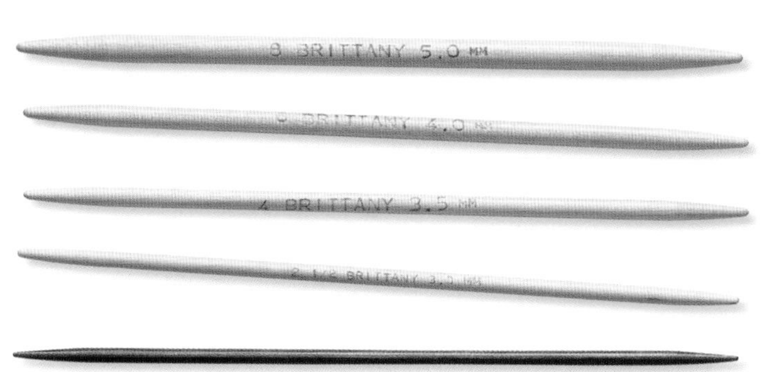

Brittany and Harmony double-pointed needles

Sets of Double-Pointed Needles

Double-pointed needles are sold in packages of four, five, or six needles (only Harmony needles comes in sets of six—an extra in case you lose or break one). I've listed a set of five needles in the materials list for each garment. While the majority of the Basic Baby Suit is knit with just four needles—three to hold the stitches and one for knitting—there is one area where five needles are necessary: when joining the legs.

The hood of the Basic Baby Suit is a little easier to knit on straight needles. It's knit back and forth, and the first section is a little too wide to fit comfortably on the 5"-long needles. If you have straight needles in the appropriate size, use them for this part. If you don't have them, don't buy them just for this project. Put some needle tips or rubber bands on one end of two double-point needles and use them. The stitches will be crowded, but there's only 1½" of knitting before some of the stitches are bound off.

Crochet Hooks

I find it is easier to pick up stitches with a crochet hook and put them on a knitting needle rather then pick them up with a knitting needle (see "Picking Up Stitches" on page 12). The wigs may also be crocheted instead of knitted.

Knitting Techniques

All of the projects in this book are intermediate in difficulty. There are some specific techniques that will be useful in knitting these small garments. Many of these techniques have to do with shaping. In designing the garments, I shape the pieces while knitting, instead of knitting several shapes and sewing them together. As much as possible, the garments are knit as one piece, except for sewing the hood in place.

KNITTING IN THE ROUND

It's helpful to know how to knit in the round using four double-pointed needles. Knitting in the round using a long circular needle is a very popular way to knit socks, but it doesn't work as well when knitting such small pieces as these doll clothes.

Joining in the Round

There are a few different ways to join stitches for knitting in the round. One of the simplest and least visible is the crossover join.

1. Cast on the correct number of stitches and distribute them evenly on three double-pointed needles. Use the fourth needle to knit stitches.

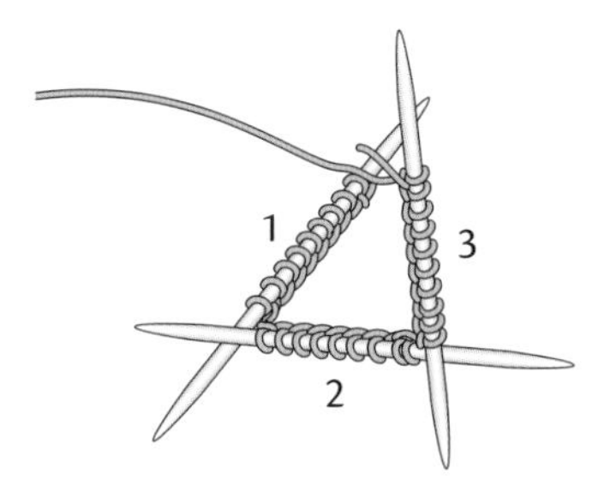

2. Hold the needles in position to begin knitting. Be sure that the row of stitches is not twisted. With the right-hand needle, slip the first stitch off the left-hand needle and place it on the right needle.
3. Using the left-hand needle, pick up the second stitch on the right-hand needle and place it on the left needle.

You've just switched the placement of the first and last stitches, joining the row for knitting in the round.

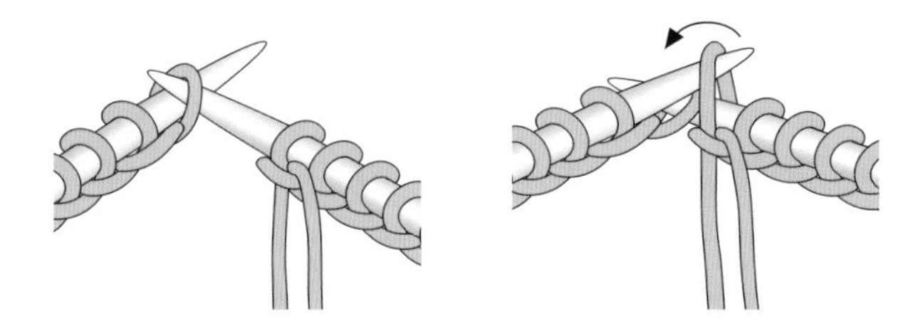

INCREASES

Two types of increases are used for the patterns in this book.

Make-One Increase (M1)

This increase is about as invisible as an increase can be.

1. Hold the working yarn to the back of the work and the two knitting needles slightly apart.

2. Using the left-hand needle, insert the tip from front to back under the horizontal yarn that runs between the stitches on the left and right needles, and pick up this yarn to make a stitch.

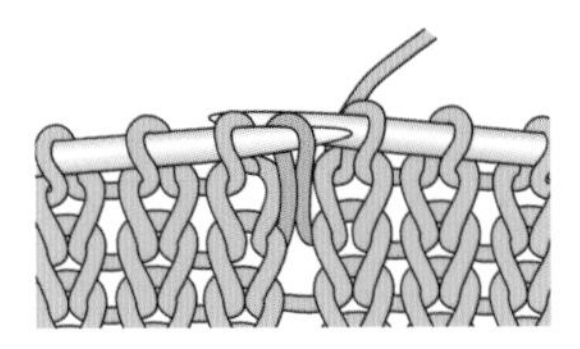

3. Knit into the back of the stitch you just picked up. Knitting into the back twists the stitch, preventing a hole from forming.

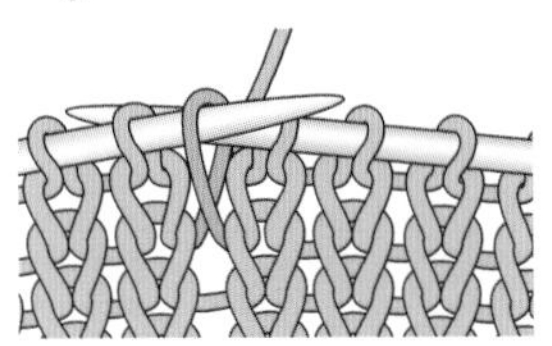

Knit in Front and Back (K1f&b)

This increase isn't as invisible as the make one, since it leaves a little bar on the right side. But it works well in some situations.

1. Knit into the stitch on the left needle but don't drop the stitch off the needle.

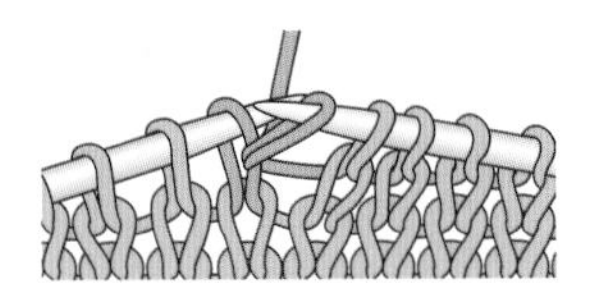

2. Knit into the back of the same stitch, and then drop it off the left needle, creating two stitches from one stitch.

THREE-NEEDLE BIND OFF (3-NEEDLE BO)

This technique allows you to join two pieces and bind them off in one step. Each of the pieces is on a separate needle, and a third needle is used to knit the stitches together and bind them off.

1. Line up the two pieces with right sides together and the needles parallel, with the stitches close to the needle tips.
2. Insert a third needle into the first stitch on the front needle and into the first stitch on the back needle, and knit these two stitches together as if they were one.

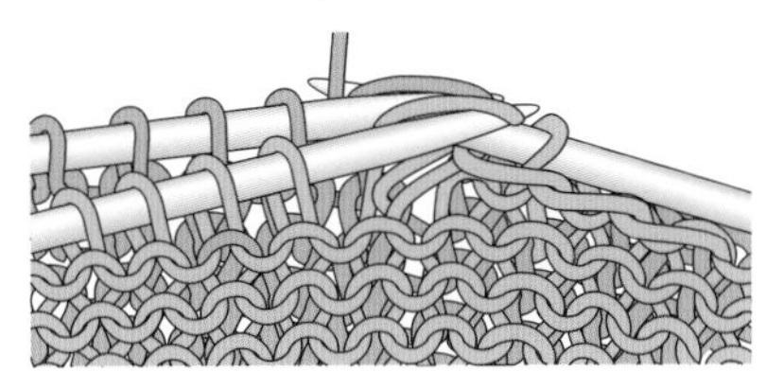

3. Repeat step 2 with the next stitches on the front and back needles. There will be two stitches on the right needle.
4. On the right needle, pass the second stitch over the first, binding it off.

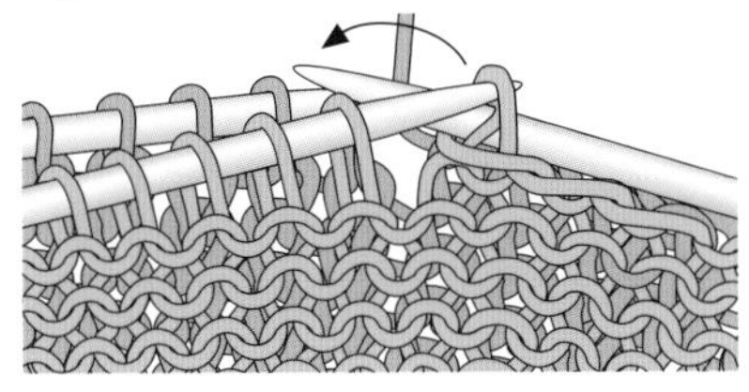

Continue knitting two stitches into one as described, and binding them off until one stitch remains. Fasten off the last stitch.

PICKING UP STITCHES

This technique is used for adding stitches to make another section of the garment, often a placket or a sleeve. Using a crochet hook to pick up stitches is a bit easier than a knitting needle in these small pieces. Picking up and knitting makes a neater join than knitting the section separately and then sewing it in place.

Placket on Basic Baby Suit

1. Hold the yarn to be attached at the back of the piece.
2. Insert a crochet hook under the two strands of an edge stitch, wrap the yarn around the hook, and pull the yarn through.
3. Place this loop of yarn on a knitting needle and pull it tightly enough against the needle to make a comfortable stitch.
4. Repeat steps 2 and 3 for the required number of stitches. Keep the tension on the new stitches even.

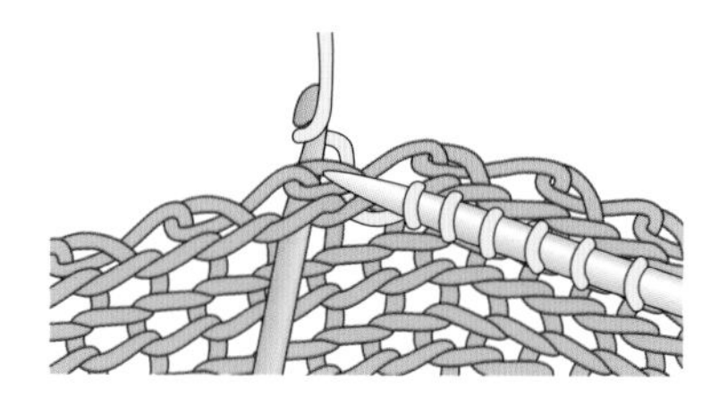

Sometimes you will skip a stitch in the rows of the knitted piece in order to pick up the correct number of stitches. (The number of stitches to be picked up is not usually the exact number of stitches in the row.) This will look uneven until you knit the first row of picked-up stitches. Then the stitches will even out.

Number of Stitches to Pick Up

Pattern instructions usually give an exact number of stitches to be picked up for a placket, sleeve, collar, etc. Everyone's knitting is different and the recommended number of stitches may not be the best for your knitting. In the instructions for the Basic Baby Suit, there are exact numbers given for the plackets, neckbands, and sleeves. The number of sleeve stitches should not be varied, but feel free to use whatever number of stitches fits best for the plackets and neckbands. It's important that the stitches are picked up evenly and that the right and left plackets have an equal number of stitches, but the exact number doesn't really matter.

SHORT ROWS

Short rows are used in making the tails of the skunk and squirrel. Short rows are partial rows of knitting worked within a piece to give it shape. Unlike standard short rows where the instructions say "wrap and turn" at the point where the work is turned, the short rows in this book do not use the wrapping step. Simply work the given number of stitches, turn the work, and knit back to the beginning of the row.

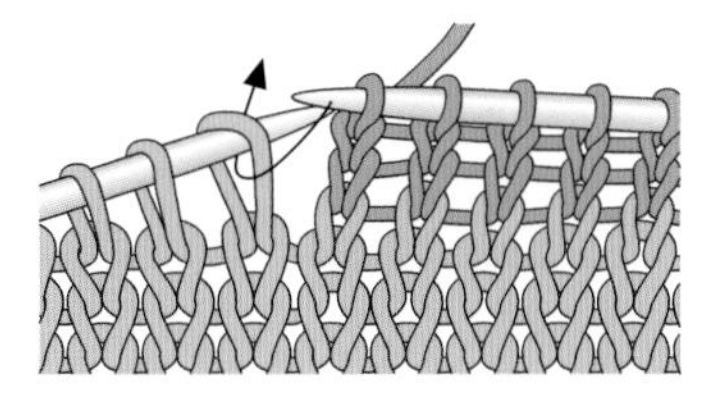

SEAMING

The Basic Baby Suit was designed to have a minimum amount of seaming. However, the bottoms of the feet have to be sewn closed, the sides of the hood are sewn to shape the hood, and the hood is sewn into place on the neckline. The Lacy Dress has a little seaming at the underarm. The most attractive-looking seaming methods are the mattress stitch on finished edges and the Kitchener stitch on live stitches.

Mattress Stitch

This method is used to seam finished edges together. The horizontal-to-horizontal stitch is used to close the feet of the Basic Baby Suit and to join the back of the hood to the neckline. The vertical-to-horizontal stitch is used for the seam that shapes the hood and the seam that joins the sides of the hood to the neckline. The finished line of stitching should blend in like a row of knitting. Sometimes you will have to skip a stitch on one edge or the other in order to get the seam to line up evenly at the end.

Horizontal to horizontal. With right sides facing up, place bound-off edges together and line up the stitches. Insert the tapestry needle under an entire stitch (which is actually two strands of yarn) from one edge, and then under the corresponding stitch on the other edge, and pull them together. Don't pull too tightly or the line will stiffen and be more visible. Continue working from one edge to the other until the seam is complete.

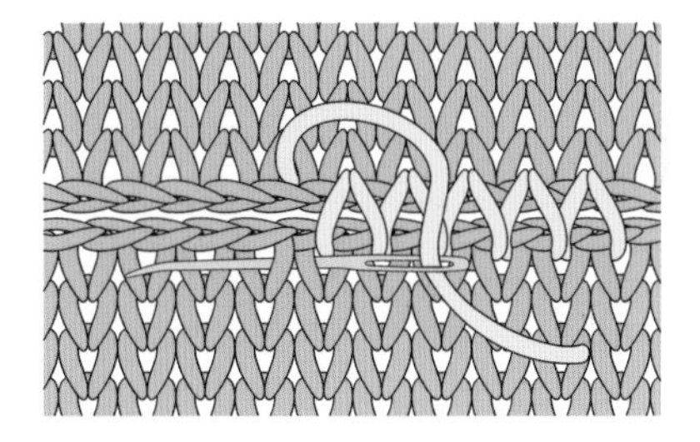

Vertical to horizontal. With right sides facing up, place the vertical bound-off edge next to the horizontal stitches. Insert the tapestry needle under an entire stitch on the vertical piece and under two horizontal bars on the horizontal piece. Pull them together, but don't pull too tightly. Continue working from one edge to the other until the seam is complete.

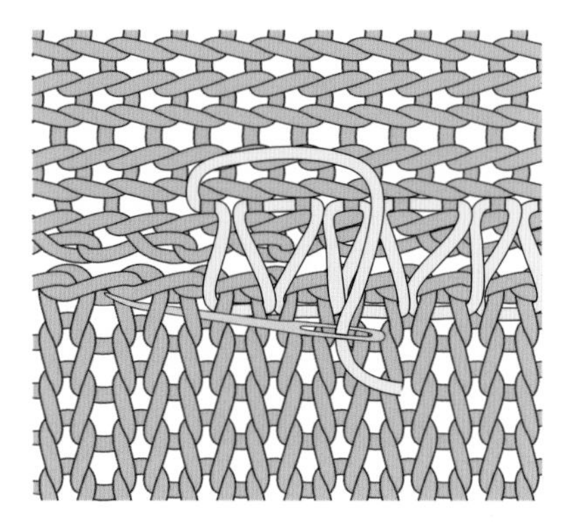

Kitchener Stitch

Use this method to sew the feet of the tights closed and to close the underarm seam of the Lacy Dress. Arrange the live stitches on two parallel needles with wrong sides together and with the working yarn coming from the back needle. There should be an equal number of stitches on each needle. Break off the working yarn, leaving at least a 12" tail. Thread this tail through a tapestry needle.

1. Insert the tapestry needle through the first stitch on the front needle as if to knit; remove the stitch from the needle.
2. Insert the tapestry needle through the next stitch on the front needle as if to purl. Pull the yarn all the way though the stitch. Leave the stitch on the needle.
3. Insert the tapestry needle through the first stitch on the back needle as if to purl; remove the stitch from the needle.
4. Insert the tapestry needle through the second stitch on the back needle as if to knit. Leave the stitch on the needle.

Repeat steps 1–4 until the last stitch. Draw the yarn through the last stitch and fasten off. Weave in the yarn tail.

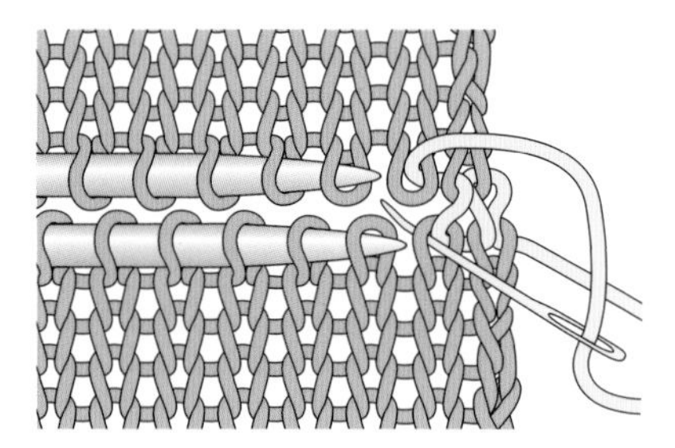

I-CORD

I-cord is a narrow tube of knitting that can be made on a device called a knitting spool, or knit with two double-pointed needles. It has many uses. It can be sewn onto a garment for embellishment or edging. It can be used for drawstrings for bags or made into decorative closures. In this book, I-cord is used as tails on the animal costumes.

To work, cast on the required number of stitches on a double-pointed needle. Do not turn the work. Slide the stitches to the right-hand end of the needle and put that needle in your left hand (or vice versa for left-handers). *Knit the stitches, pulling the yarn snugly as you knit. Do not turn the work. Slide the stitches to the opposite end of the needle. Repeat from * until the I-cord is the desired length.

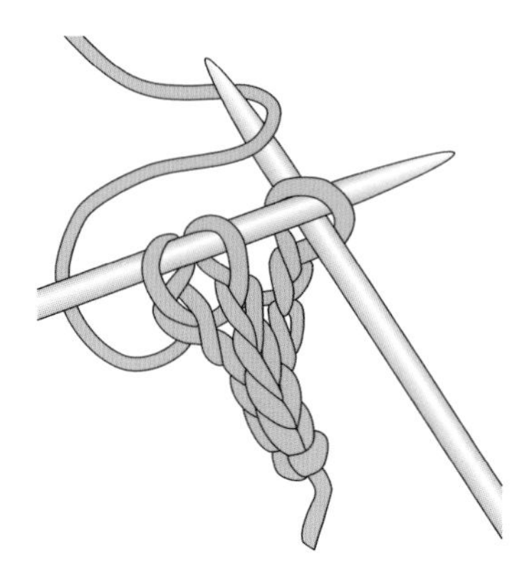

WEAVING IN YARN TAILS

I was a knitter for a very long time before I learned the best way to weave in yarn tails. There's no perfect way to deal with these little pests, but the goal is to prevent them from working their way to the front of your otherwise flawless knitting.

I find that the best way to do this is to make a duplicate stitch for three or four horizontal stitches on the right side of the knitting. Leave about 8" of yarn tail before you cut it and bring it to the right side of the work.

Thread the tail on a tapestry needle and follow a row of already knit stitches by inserting the needle under the base of the knit stitch directly above the stitch to be duplicated. Then reinsert the needle at the base of the duplicated stitch (the same place it emerged initially). Repeat for three or four more stitches. Then take the yarn to the wrong side and work about ½" of yarn diagonally across a few stitches. Cut the yarn, leaving a ½" tail or so.

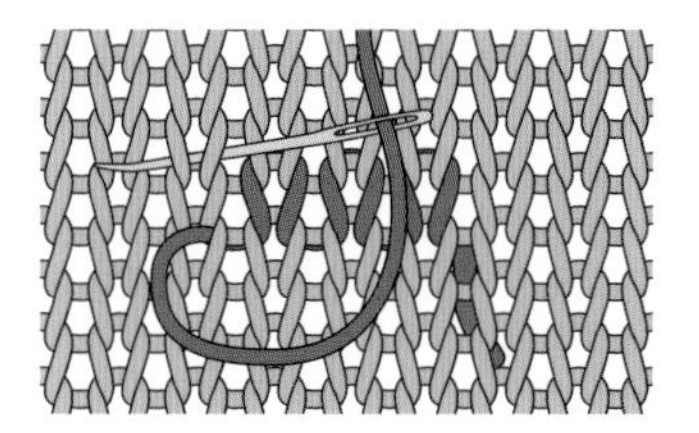

The duplicate stitch is often used to add decoration, but when the working yarn is the same as the background, the stitches blend in.

Doll front
Doll back
Finished doll

Baby Whimsy Doll

This cute doll is the perfect size for little hands to play with, and provides older hands with the opportunity to make adorable small-sized knitting projects.

SIZE

9" from head to toes

MATERIALS FOR BODY

⅛ yard of medium-weight woven fabric (45" wide) in color of your choice

Thread to match fabric

Polyester stuffing

Embroidery floss for eyes and mouth and embroidery needle

Pencil

Pins

Hand-sewing needles

Wooden chopstick or small dowel

Freezer paper (optional; available in supermarkets where the food wraps are)

See page 21 for hair materials and instructions.

Pattern Alert!

Contrary to most sewing patterns, these pattern pieces are not cut from the fabric until *after* the seams are sewn. Be sure to read the instructions thoroughly before starting.

TRANSFERRING THE PATTERNS TO FABRIC

Note that you'll need only one pattern piece for the body of the doll. Don't cut out separate pattern pieces for the front and back. Cut out one full body pattern piece, initially ignoring the cutting line for the front lower piece. The lower front will be cut after sewing the front and back pieces together.

Also note that there are no lines designating the grain of the fabric. You can cut the body pieces along the grain of the fabric, but grain doesn't matter for the arms and legs.

1. Photocopy or trace the pattern pieces from page 23 onto unlined paper or freezer paper. Freezer paper has a plastic coating on one side that lightly adheres to fabric when it's ironed. The advantage of using freezer paper is that you don't have to trace the pattern shapes onto the fabric. You iron the pattern pieces onto the fabric. The freezer-paper pieces can be used repeatedly, which saves you time if you're making more than one doll.
2. Cut out the pattern pieces from the paper along the outer lines. Do not leave a seam allowance on the pattern pieces.

3. Place the pieces on the wrong side of the fabric, leaving at least ½" between them to allow for cutting seam allowances. If you're using regular paper, trace around the pattern pieces using a sharp pencil to draw directly onto the fabric. If you're using freezer paper, place the plastic-coated side down toward the fabric and iron the pieces in place with a medium hot iron. Leave the freezer-paper pieces adhered to the fabric until after sewing. There's no need to trace around the freezer-paper pieces.
4. Place the marked fabric on a second layer of fabric, with right sides together. Do not cut the fabric yet.

SEWING

Set the sewing machine to sew very small stitches (15 to 20 stitches per inch). Using thread to match the fabric, sew directly on the drawn lines or on the edge of the freezer paper. Sew only on the seam lines as illustrated on the pattern. Do not sew along the dotted or dashed lines. Backstitch at both ends of the seam lines so the stitches don't pull out when you turn the pieces right side out.

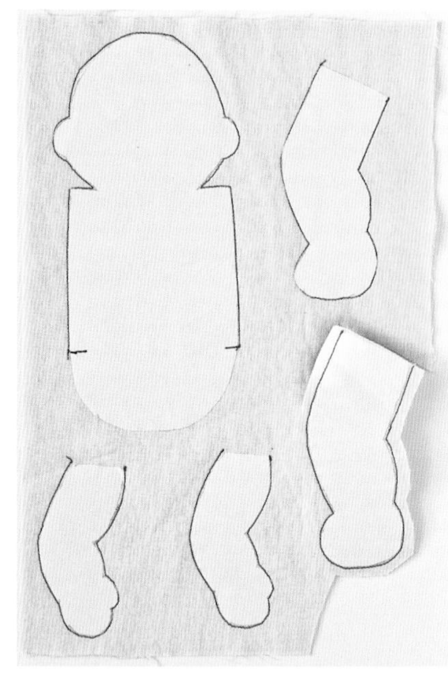

Freezer-paper patterns ironed onto fabric. Red thread is used for demonstration purposes only to make the seam lines more visible. One of the legs is partially cut out, leaving an appropriate seam allowance.

CUTTING AND STUFFING

Cut the pieces out, leaving ⅛"-wide seam allowances along solid and dashed lines. Cut the bottom front on the dotted line as indicated, without leaving a seam allowance. Snip inner angles close to the stitching.

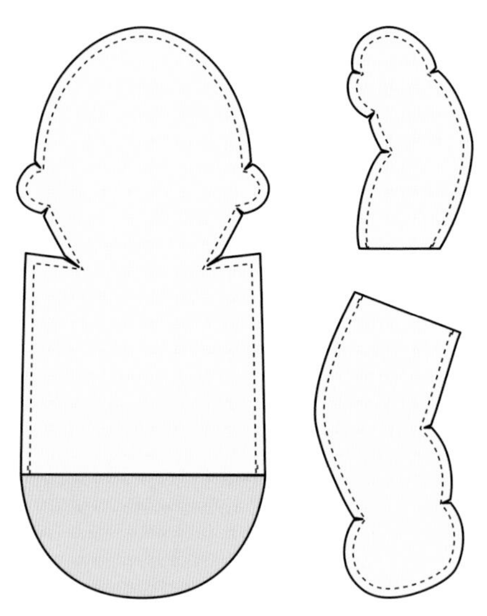

Head and Body

Turn the head/body inside out and run the edge of the chopstick along the inside of the seams to flatten them. Place a very small amount of stuffing in the ears, pressing the stuffing in place with the chopstick.

Machine stitch along the inside of the ear, still using the short-stitch setting. Be careful not to extend this stitching beyond the ear; this will distort the shape of the face.

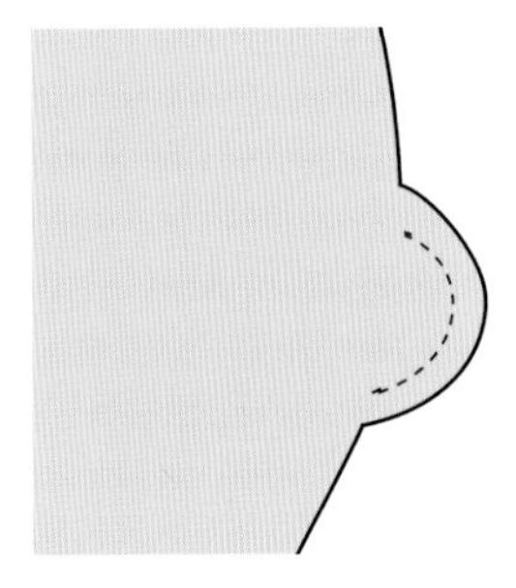

Stitching the Ear

Since this is such a small area of stitching, it may be necessary to move the machine wheel by hand to stitch very slowly around the curve of the ear. Place the needle in the down position, raise the presser foot, move the fabric as necessary. Take a stitch. Repeat until the curve is done. Remember to backstitch at the beginning and end of this short line of stitching.

Legs and Arms

Turn the pieces right side out and press the seams flat with the chopstick. Firmly stuff the pieces, using very small amounts of stuffing at a time and pushing the stuffing in with the blunt end of the chopstick. When the pieces are adequately stuffed, fold in the top edges ⅛". For the legs, line up the front and back seams in the center. For the arms, the seams are on the sides of the pieces. Pin to hold each piece closed. Whipstitch each piece closed using small stitches.

Closing the Body

Firmly stuff the head and body. Turn the lower back edge approximately ⅛" toward the inside. Hem this edge by hand using a running stitch. At the end of the hem, pull the thread to slightly gather the back edge. Fold the lower back of the doll so that the gathered edge meets the front edge. Sew it to the front edge using a whipstitch to close the body.

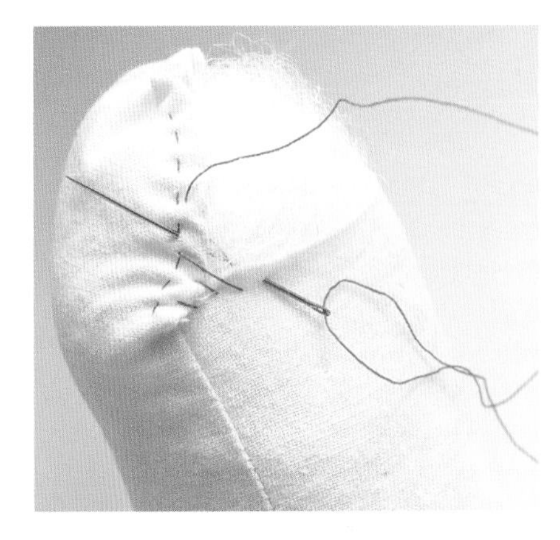

JOINING LIMBS

On the finished doll, the limbs should fold in toward the front of the doll. To accomplish this, hold the limb in place against the front of the doll while you attach it from the back side of the doll. Hand stitch the arms on the side seams, even with the top of the shoulders. Sew the legs on the back gathered seam, with the outside of the legs even with the side seams; there should be a ¼" to ½" space in the middle between the legs.

Securing Limbs

Double stitch the seams attaching the limbs to the body for extra durability.

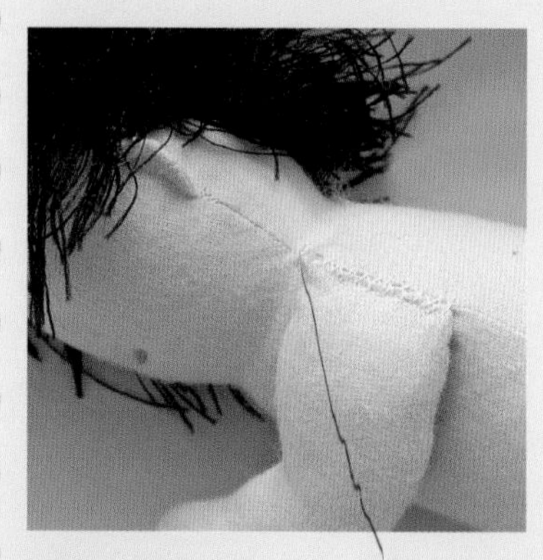

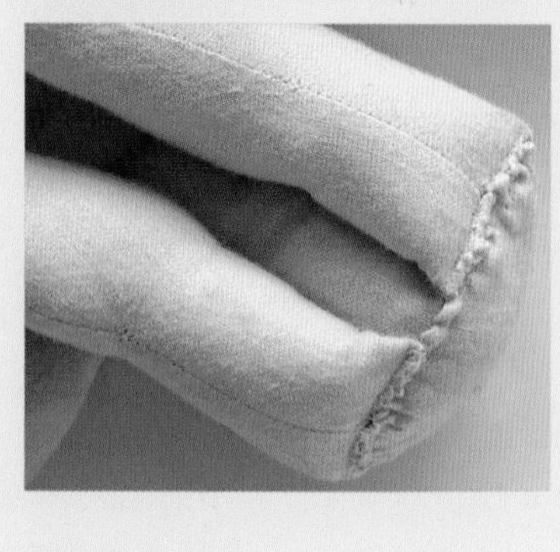

EMBROIDERING THE FACE

The eyes and mouth are stitched with embroidery floss. Mark the eyes and nose placement with pins, and then use a pencil to lightly mark where the pins are; remove the pins. Note that the embroidery is done after stuffing the doll. This is so you have the full shape of the face to work with and can see better where to place the features; this can be difficult to do on a flat, unstuffed piece.

Placing Mouth and Eyes

Imagine two lines across the doll's face, one between the tops of the ears and one between the bottoms of the ears. The mouth should be placed along the bottom line and the eyes along the top line. This is how it is on your own face.

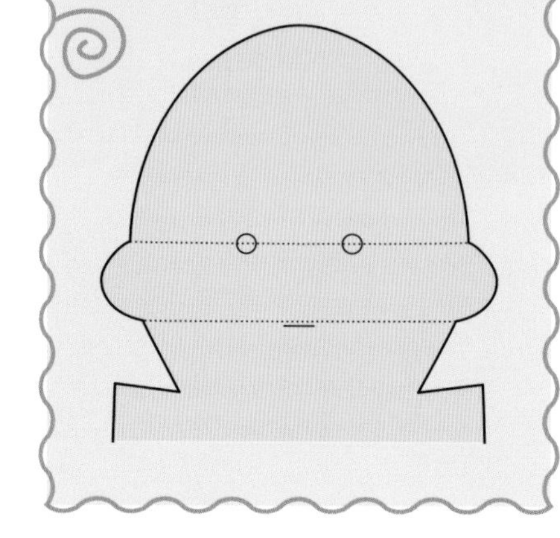

Mouth

Use all six strands of embroidery floss. Cut a piece of floss approximately 8" long and make a knot at one end. Insert the needle from the back of the head to the front where the mouth should be. Make one stitch about ¼" long, and then insert the needle into the front and pull through to the back. Fasten off on the back of the head. The hair will cover the knots.

Eyes

Using two stands of embroidery floss, cut a piece of thread approximately 12" long and make a knot at one end. Insert the needle from the back of the head to the front where the first eye should be. Use satin stitches to make the eye. Then insert the yarn back into the head and come up where the next eye should be, going under the stuffing a little bit so the dark thread doesn't show through. Make another satin-stitch eye. The challenge is to get the eyes lined up properly and as close to the same shape as possible. You may want to practice this on piece of scrap fabric first. Fasten the thread off on the back of the head.

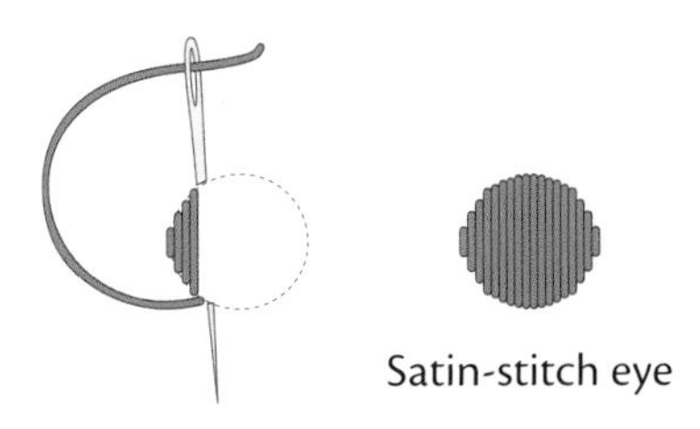
Satin-stitch eye

HAIR

Materials

Note that Splash, Fun Fur, and Boa look better when knitted. Allure and Fizz look better when crocheted. The following are suggested needle and hook sizes for these yarns. If you use another brand of novelty yarn, you will have to experiment with needle and hook sizes to get the required 4" pieces. See photo on page 7 for examples of suitable yarns for doll hair.

Approx 6 yards of Lion Brand Yarn Fun Fur, Patons Allure, Bernat Boa, or Crystal Palace Yarns Splash OR 12 yards of Crystal Palace Yarns Fizz.

Sewing needle and thread to match yarn.

For knitted hair:

Size 8 (5 mm) needles for Splash*

Size 10 (6 mm) needles for Fun Fur or Boa*

For crocheted hair:

Size G-6 (6.5 mm) hook for Fizz*

Size N-15 (10 mm) hook for Allure*

**Or size required to make a 4"-diameter circle.*

The goal is to produce a round shape no more than 4" in diameter and thick enough that the fabric of the doll's head doesn't show through when the hair is sewn in place. It can be crocheted or knit. You may have to experiment with your yarn using different size needles or hooks to get the appropriate size. Some yarns look better knitted; some are better crocheted.

Knitted hair in Crystal Palace Yarns Splash on the top. Crocheted hair in Patons Allure on the bottom.

Crocheted Hair

An advantage to crocheting the hair is that you can make it exactly the size you want. The disadvantage is that it's difficult to see the stitches when you crochet with novelty yarn. If you can't see exactly where you should insert the hook, just poke it in the approximate stitch. Even if it's in the wrong place, it won't show.

Use the size of crochet hook appropriate for your yarn.

Ch 4, sl st to join in a circle.

Rnd 1: Sc 6 in the circle.

Rnd 2 and subsequent rnds: (Sc 1, 2 sc in next sc), repeat around and around until piece is 4" in diameter.

The piece may be dome shaped or flat. Try the wig on the doll as you work. When it looks good to you, fasten off the last stitch.

Knitted Hair

Because people knit with different tensions, the needle sizes that I used may not give you the same results. If the knitted wig turns out to be a little short of 4" diameter, try it on the doll and see if it can be stretched without the fabric showing through. Use the size of needles appropriate for your yarn. If it needs to be larger, go up a needle size or two. If the wig is more than 4", go down a needle size.

CO 7 sts.

Rows 1 and 2: Knit.

Row 3: K1f&b, knit to last st, K1f&b—9 sts.

Rows 4–9: Rep rows 1–3 twice more—13 sts.

Rows 10 and 11: Knit.

Row 12: K2tog, knit to last 2 sts, K2tog—11 sts.

Rows 13–18: Rep rows 10–12 twice more—7 sts.

Row 19: Knit.

BO all sts and weave in ends.

Attaching Hair

Attach the hair to the doll's head by stitching around the edge of the piece along what would be the hairline on a person. It's not necessary to stitch the hair to the top of the head. As you stitch the hair in place you can fudge a little here and there to give it the proper shape. This is one of those things that you can do imperfectly and it will still work out. The finished knitted or crocheted hair can look a bit misshapen beforehand and yet look perfect when it's on the doll. I crocheted my first doll's hair and I don't know how to crochet, so I know about misshapen doll hair!

Patterns shown actual size.

—— Sew on solid line, then cut, leaving ⅛" seam allowance.

- - - - Cut ⅛" from dashed line for added seam allowance.

·········· Cut on dotted line, leaving no seam allowance.

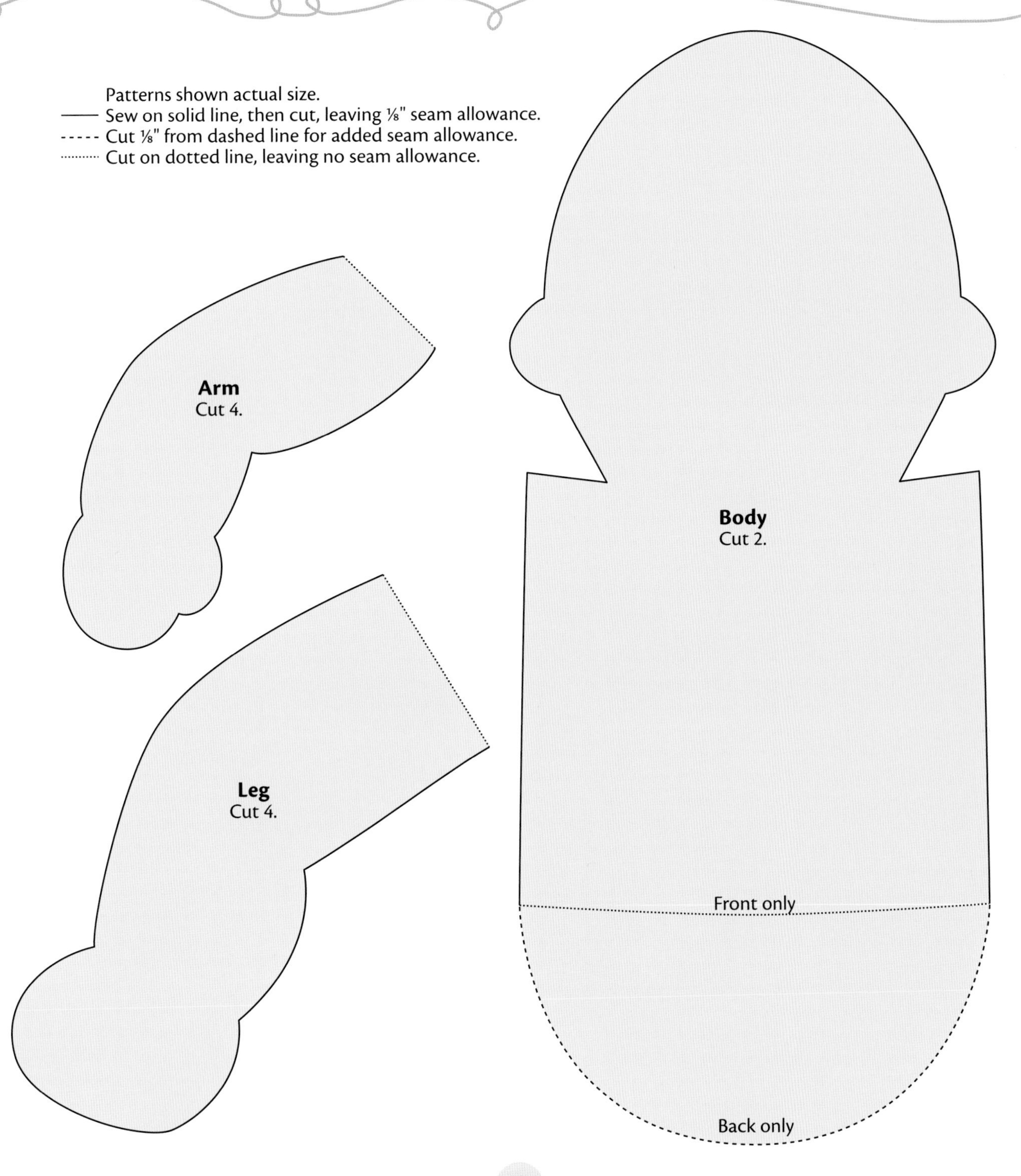

Suits from left to right: fingering-, DK-, and sport-weight yarn

Basic Baby Suit

Instructions are given to make the Basic Baby Suit in three different weights of yarn—fingering, sport, and DK. This garment can be varied in many ways. It can be made with or without a hood, or with or without feet. You can vary the length of the sleeves and legs. You can use a contrasting color for the ribbing and plackets if you like. This suit is the basis for all the animal costumes. The foot is the fiddliest part of this project; you may want to do a practice foot and leg as a gauge swatch.

BASIC BABY SUIT IN FINGERING-WEIGHT YARN

Yarns Used

Suit: Knit Picks Palette in colors Blue and Sky.

Doll hair: Patons Allure in color Ebony.

Size

Body length: Approx 6½" from shoulder to feet; length without feet as desired

Materials

MC Partial 50 g ball of fingering-weight yarn

CC 5 yards of fingering-weight yarn

Set of 5 size 2 (2.75 mm) double-pointed needles, 5" or 6" long

Size 2 (2.75 mm) straight needles (optional) for making hood

Size D-3 (3.25 mm) crochet hook

2 small stitch holders

Waste yarn to hold stitches

Tapestry needle

3 buttons, ⅜" to ½" diameter

Gauge

8 sts = 1" in St st

Legs without Feet

For a baby suit with feet, skip to *"Left Foot and Leg" on page 26.*

*With MC, CO 28 sts. Distribute sts on 3 needles, join in rnd. If using CC, CO and work ribbing in CC, then switch to MC.

Work 4 rnds in K1, P1 ribbing.

M1 st in next rnd (29 sts) and work piece until desired length of leg.

When leg is desired length, knit first 3 sts of rnd and leave on needle. Place all other sts on waste yarn. Using rem 4 dpns, rep from * for second leg.

Skip to "Joining Legs" at right.

Left Foot and Leg

With MC, CO 16 sts. Distribute sts on 3 needles, join in rnd. Intersection of needles 1 and 3 is heel of foot. Needle 2 holds toe sts.

Rnd 1: Knit.

Rnd 2: K1, M1, K3, M1, K4, M1, K4, M1, K3, M1, K1–21 sts.

Rnd 3: K1, M1, K9, M1, K1, M1, K9, M1, K1–25 sts.

Rnd 4: K11, M1, K3, M1, K11–27 sts.

Rnd 5: K11, M1, K5, M1, K11–29 sts.

Rnd 6: Knit.

Rnd 7: Knit.

Rnd 8: K11, ssk, K3, K2tog, K11–27 sts.

Rnd 9: K11, ssk, K1, K2tog, K11–25 sts.

Rnd 10: K11, sl 1-K2tog-psso, K11–23 sts.

Rnd 11: Knit.

Rnd 12: K1, ssk, K6, K2tog, K1, ssk, K6, K2tog, K1–19 sts.

Rnd 13: Knit.

Rnd 14: K1, M1, (K2, M1) 4 times, K1, M1, (K2, M1) 4 times, K1–29 sts.

Knit even until piece measures 3¼".

Leg Join

In last rnd of knitting each leg, leave 3 sts on single needle and place all other sts on waste yarn. The sts on needle are center 3 sts of each inner leg. The leg join will be worked using these 6 sts. Note that last rnd of knitting is different for left and right legs because these center sts fall in a different part of rnd for each leg.

Last rnd of left leg: Knit an incomplete rnd, stopping when 5 sts rem at end of rnd. Leave last 3 sts worked on needle. Place all other sts on waste yarn. Cut working yarn, leaving about 10" tail.

Right Foot and Leg

Work as for left foot and leg until piece measures 3¼".

Last rnd of right leg: Knit first 8 sts of rnd and stop. Leave last 3 sts worked on needle. Place all other sts on waste yarn. Do not cut off working yarn.

Joining Legs

Hold the 2 legs together, needles parallel with 3 sts on each needle and right leg closest to you The toes of both legs should be pointing in same direction. The working sts should be on inner side of legs, and working yarn attached to right leg. With a third needle, work 3-needle BO (page 11). There will be 1 st left on needle. Pick up all sts from waste yarn on both legs, distributing them on 4 dpns, arranging them so st rem from leg join is last st in rnd–53 sts. Note that there will be holes at each end of leg join. These will be sewn closed when you finish garment. The next few rnds can be awkward to knit because leg join prevents piece from being circular. Distributing sts on 4 dpns and working with fifth needle makes it easier. Each row above leg join gets progressively easier to work.

Body

Knit around until piece measures 1" from leg join.

BO center-front 3 sts and knit back and forth in St st until piece measures 1¾" from leg join—50 sts.

Divide for Fronts and Back

Divide sts as follows: 12 sts on needle 1 for right front, 26 sts on needle 2 for back, 12 sts on needle 3 for left front.

Left front: Knit left front until piece measures 2¾" from leg join. (BO 3 sts at neck edge, work to end, work next row) twice. Place rem 6 sts on holder.

Right front: Work as for left front.

Back

Work 26 back sts in St st until even with second row of bound-off sts on front.

Next row: K6, BO 14 sts, knit to end.

Turn garment inside out. Work 3-needle BO to join front and back shoulders.

Sleeves

Using crochet hook for pickup (page 12) and MC, PU 28 sts around sleeve opening.

Knit in rnd in St st until sleeve measures 1⅜" from pickup row. If using CC for ribbing, switch to CC and knit 1 rnd before beg ribbing.

Work 3 rnds in K1, P1 ribbing.

BO all sts in patt.

Garment without Hood

Skip to "Garment with Hood" at right if you want to add hood.

Neckband

Using crochet hook and MC or CC, PU 34 sts around neck edge. If using CC for ribbing, switch to CC.

Work 3 rows in K1, P1 ribbing.

BO all sts in patt.

Left Placket

Using crochet hook and MC or CC, PU 20 sts along left edge of opening, including edge of neckband.

Row 1: Work K1, P1 ribbing.

Row 2 (buttonholes): K1, P1, YO, K2tog, (work 5 sts, YO, K2tog) twice, K1, P1.

Rows 3 and 4: Work K1, P1 ribbing.

BO all sts in patt.

Right Placket

PU 20 sts along right edge of opening.

Work 4 rows in K1, P1 ribbing.

BO all sts in patt.

Garment with Hood

Left Placket

Using crochet hook and MC or CC, PU 18 sts along left edge of opening.

Row 1: Work K1, P1 ribbing.

Row 2 (buttonholes): K1, P1, YO, K2tog, (work 4 sts, YO, K2tog) twice, K1, P1.

Rows 3 and 4: Work K1, P1 ribbing.

BO all sts in patt.

Right Placket

PU 18 sts along right edge of opening.

Work 4 rows in K1, P1 ribbing.

BO all sts in patt.

Hood

You can use straight or circular needles for this step. The width of piece is approx 6½" and can be worked on a short pair of dpns. See page 9 for adapting dpns.

Using straight needles and MC or CC, CO 52 sts.

Work 4 rows in K1, P1 ribbing.

Switch to MC if you started with CC, work in St st until piece measures 1½" from CO.

Next 2 rows: BO 18 sts, work to end.

Work rem 16 sts in St st until piece measures 4" from CO.

BO all sts.

Sew side seams of hood as shown. Sew hood to neckline, excluding top of placket.

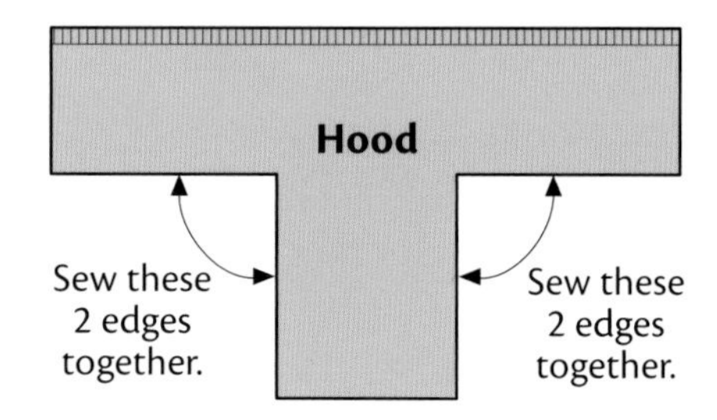

Finishing

Using yarn tails, sew bottom end of placket in place, close holes at leg join, and sew bottom of feet closed using mattress st (page 13). Sew 3 buttons to right placket opposite buttonholes. Weave in yarn tails.

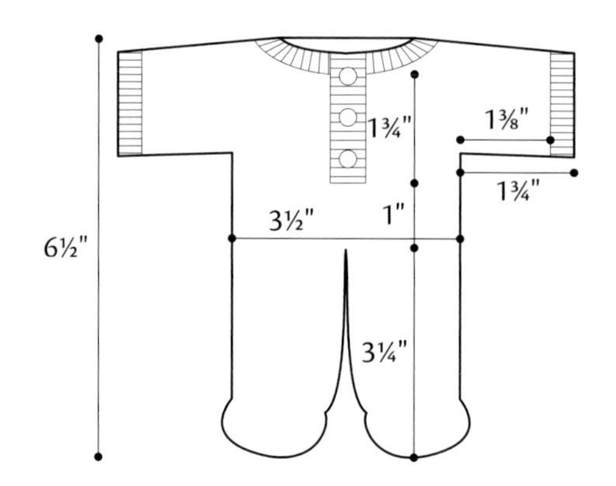

BASIC BABY SUIT IN SPORT-WEIGHT YARN

Yarns Used

Suit: Frog Tree Yarns Alpaca Sport Melange in colors 919 dark green and 913 light green.
Doll hair: Crystal Palace Yarns Splash in color 9149.

Size

Body length: Approx 6½" from shoulder to toes

Materials

MC Partial 50 g ball of sport-weight yarn

CC 4 yds of sport-weight yarn

Set of 5 size 4 (3.5 mm) double-point needles, 5" or 6" long

Size 4 (3.5 mm) straight needles (optional) for making hood

Size E-4 (3.5 mm) crochet hook

2 small stitch holders

Tapestry needle

Waste yarn to hold stitches

3 buttons, ⅜" to ½" diameter

Gauge

6 sts = 1" in St st

Legs without Feet

For a baby suit with feet, skip to "Left Foot and Leg" below.

*With MC, CO 22 sts. Distribute sts on 3 needles and join in rnd. If using CC, CO and work ribbing in CC, then switch to MC.

Work 3 rnds in K1, P1 ribbing.

M1 st in next rnd (23 sts) and work piece until desired length of leg.

When leg is desired length, knit first 2 sts of rnd and leave on needle. Place all other sts on waste yarn. Using rem 4 dpns, rep from * for second leg.

Skip to "Joining Legs" at right.

Left Foot and Leg

With MC, CO 14 sts. Distribute sts on 3 needles and join in rnd. Intersection of needles 1 and 3 is heel of foot. Needle 2 holds toe sts.

Rnd 1: Knit.

Rnd 2: K1, M1, K6, M1, K6, M1, K1–17 sts.

Rnd 3: K8, M1, K1, M1, K8–19 sts.

Rnd 4: K8, M1, K3, M1, K8–21 sts.

Rnd 5: Knit.

Rnd 6: K8, ssk, K1, K2tog, K8–19 sts.

Rnd 7: K8, sl 1-K2tog-psso, K8–17 sts.

Rnd 8: K1, ssk, K11, K2tog, K1–15 sts.

Rnds 9 and 10: Knit.

Rnd 11: K1, (M1, K2) 3 times, M1, K1, (M1, K2) 3 times, M1, K1–23 sts.

Knit even until piece measures 3¼".

Leg Join

In last rnd of knitting each leg, you'll leave 2 sts on single needle and place all other sts on waste yarn. The sts on needle are center 2 sts of each inner leg. The leg join will be worked using these 4 sts. Note that last rnd of knitting is different for left and right legs because these center sts fall in a different part of rnd for each leg.

Last rnd of left leg: Knit incomplete rnd, stopping when 4 sts rem at end of rnd. Leave last 2 sts worked on needle. Place all other sts on waste yarn. Cut working yarn, leaving about 10" tail.

Right Foot and Leg

Work as for left foot and leg until piece measures 3¼".

Last rnd of right leg: Knit first 6 sts of rnd and stop. Leave last 2 sts worked on needle. Place all other sts on waste yarn. Do not cut off working yarn.

Joining Legs

Hold the two legs together, needles parallel with 2 sts on each needle and right leg closest to you. The toes of both legs should be pointing in the same direction. The working sts should be on inner side of legs, and working yarn attached to right leg. With a third needle, work 3-needle BO (page 11). There will be 1 st left on needle. Pick up all sts from waste yarn on both legs, distributing them on 4 dpns, arranging them so rem st from leg join is last st in rnd–43 sts. Note that there will be holes at each end of leg join. These will be sewn closed when you finish garment. The next few rnds can be awkward to knit because leg join prevents piece from being circular. Distributing sts on 4 dpns and working with fifth needle makes it easier. Each row above leg join gets progressively easier to work.

Body

Knit in rnd until piece measures 1" from leg join.

BO center front 2 sts and knit back and forth in St st until piece measures 1¾" from leg join—41 sts.

Divide for Fronts and Back

Divide sts as follows: 10 sts on needle 1 for right front, 21 sts on needle 2 for back, 10 sts on needle 3 for left front.

Left front: Knit left front until piece measures 2¾" from leg join. BO 3 sts at neck edge, work to end, work next row. BO 2 sts at neck edge, work to end, work next row. Place rem 5 sts on holder.

Right front: Work as for left front.

Back

Work 21 back sts in St st until even with second row of bound-off sts on front.

Next row: K5, BO 11, knit to end.

Turn garment inside out. Work 3-needle BO to join front and back shoulders.

Sleeves

Using crochet hook for pickup (page 12) and MC, PU 22 sts around sleeve opening.

Knit in rnd in St st until sleeve measures 1⅜" from pickup row. If using CC for ribbing, switch to CC and knit 1 rnd before beg ribbing.

Work 3 rnds in K1, P1 ribbing

BO all sts in patt.

Garment without Hood

Skip to "Garment with Hood" at right if you want to add a hood.

Neckband

Using crochet hook and MC or CC, PU 28 sts around neck edge.

Work 3 rows in K1, P1 ribbing.

BO all sts in patt.

Left Placket

Using crochet hook and MC or CC, PU 14 sts along left edge of opening, including edge of neckband.

Row 1: Work K1, P1 ribbing.

Row 2 (buttonholes): K1, P1, K1, YO, K2tog, (work 2 sts, YO, K2tog) twice, work last st.

Row 3: Work K1, P1 ribbing.

BO all sts in patt.

Right Placket

PU 14 sts along right edge of opening

Work 3 rows in K1, P1 ribbing.

BO all sts in patt.

Garment with Hood

Left Placket

Using crochet hook and MC or CC, PU 12 sts along left edge of opening.

Row 1: Work K1, P1 ribbing.

Row 2 (buttonholes): K1, (YO, K2tog, P1, K1) twice, YO, K2tog, P1.

Row 3: Work K1, P1 ribbing.

BO all sts in patt.

Right Placket

PU 12 sts along right edge of opening.

Work 3 rows in K1, P1 ribbing.

BO all sts in patt.

Hood

You can use straight or circular needles for this step. The width of piece is approx 6½" and can be worked on a short pair of dpns. See page 9 for adapting dpns.

Using straight needles and MC or CC, CO 40 sts.

Work 4 rows in K1, P1 ribbing.

Switch to MC if you started with CC, work in St st until piece measures 1½" from CO.

Next 2 rows: BO 14 sts, work to end.

Work rem 12 sts in St st until piece measures 4" from CO.

BO all sts.

Sew side seams of hood as shown on page 28. Sew hood to neckline, excluding top of placket.

Finishing

Using yarn tails, sew bottom end of placket in place, close holes at leg join, and using mattress st, sew bottom of feet closed. Sew buttons to right placket opposite buttonholes. Weave in yarn tails.

BASIC BABY SUIT IN DK-WEIGHT YARN

Yarns Used

Suit: Knit Picks Crayon DK in color Begonia.
Doll hair: Crystal Palace Yarns Splash in color black.

Size

Body length: Approx 6½" from shoulder to toes

Materials

MC Partial ball of DK-weight yarn

CC 4 yds of DK-weight yarn in contrasting color (optional)

Set of 5 size 6 (4 mm) double-pointed needles, 5" or 6" long

Size 6 (4 mm) straight needles (optional) for making hood

Size E-4 (3.5 mm) crochet hook

2 small stitch holders

Waste yarn to hold stitches

Tapestry needle

3 buttons, ⅜" to ½" diameter

Gauge

5½ sts = 1" in St st

Legs without Feet

For a baby suit with feet, skip to "Left Foot and Leg" (page 32).

*With MC, CO 18 sts. Distribute sts on 3 needles and join in rnd. If using CC, CO and work ribbing in CC, then switch to MC.

Work 3 rnds in K1, P1 ribbing.

M1 st in next rnd (19 sts) and work piece until desired length of leg.

When leg is desired length, knit first 2 sts of rnd and leave them on needle. Place all other sts on waste yarn. Using rem 4 dpns, rep from * for second leg.

Skip to "Joining Legs" (page 32).

Left Foot and Leg

With MC, CO 12 sts. Distribute sts on 3 needles and join in rnd. Intersection of needles 1 and 3 is heel of foot. Needle 2 holds toe sts.

Rnd 1: Knit.

Rnd 2: M1, K6, M1, K6–14 sts.

Rnd 3: K7, M1, K1, M1, K6–16 sts.

Rnd 4: K7, M1, K3, M1, K6–18 sts.

Rnd 5: K7, ssk, K1, K2tog, K6–16 sts.

Rnd 6: K7, sl 1-K2tog-psso, K6–14 sts.

Rnd 7: K2tog, K12–13 sts.

Rnd 8: Knit.

Rnd 9: K2, (M1, K2) 5 times, M1, K1–19 sts.

Knit even until piece measures 3¼".

Last rnd of left leg: Knit an incomplete rnd, stopping when 3 sts rem at end of rnd. Leave last 2 sts worked on needle. Place all other sts on waste yarn. Cut working yarn, leaving about 10" tail.

Leg Join

In last rnd of knitting each leg you'll leave 2 sts on single needle and place all other sts on waste yarn. The sts on needle are center 2 sts of each inner leg. The leg join will be worked using these 4 sts. Note that last rnd of knitting is different for left and right legs because these center sts fall in different part of rnd for each leg.

Right Foot and Leg

Work as for left foot and leg until piece measures 3¼".

Last rnd of right leg: Knit first 5 sts of rnd and stop. Leave last 2 sts worked on needle. Place all other sts on waste yarn. Do not cut working yarn.

Joining Legs

Hold the 2 legs together, needles parallel with 2 sts on each needle and right leg closest to you. The toes of both legs should be pointing in same direction. The working sts should be on inner side of legs, and working yarn attached to right leg.

With third needle, work 3-needle BO (page 11). There will be 1 st left on needle. Pick up all sts from waste yarn on both legs, distributing them on 4 dpns, arranging them so rem st from leg join is last st in rnd–35 sts. Note that there will be holes at each end of leg join. These will be sewn closed when you finish garment. The next few rnds can be awkward to knit because leg join prevents piece from being circular. Distributing sts on 4 dpns and working with fifth needle makes it easier. Each row above leg join gets progressively easier to work.

Body

Knit in rnd until piece measures 1" from leg join.

BO 2 center-front sts and knit back and forth in St st until piece measures 1¾" from leg join.

Divide for Fronts and Back

Divide sts as follows: 8 sts on needle 1 for right front, 17 sts on needle 2 for back, 8 sts on needle 3 for left front.

Left front: Knit left front until piece measures 2¾" from leg join. (BO 2 sts at neck edge, work to end, work next row) twice. Place rem 4 sts on holder.

Right front: Work as for left front.

BACK

Work 17 back sts in St st until even with front.

Next row: Work 4 sts, BO 9 sts, work to end.

Turn garment inside out. Work 3-needle BO to join front and back shoulders.

Sleeves

Using crochet hook for pickup (page 12) and MC, PU 18 sts around sleeve opening.

Knit in rnd in St st until sleeve measures 1¼" from pickup row. If using CC for ribbing, switch to CC and knit 1 rnd before beg ribbing.

Work 2 rnds in K1, P1 ribbing.

BO all sts in patt.

Garment without Hood

Skip to "Garment with Hood" at right if you want to add hood.

Neckband

Using crochet hook and MC or CC, PU 20 sts around neck edge.

Work 2 rows in K1, P1 ribbing.

BO all sts in patt.

Left Placket

Using crochet hook and MC or CC, PU 12 sts along left edge of opening.

Row 1: Work K1, P1 ribbing.

Row 2 (buttonholes): K1, (YO, K2tog, P1, K1) twice, YO, K2tog, P1.

BO all sts in patt.

Right Placket

PU 12 sts along right edge of opening.

Work 2 rows in K1, P1 ribbing.

BO all sts in patt.

Garment with Hood

Left Placket

Using crochet hook and MC or CC, PU 10 sts along left edge of opening.

Row 1: Work K1, P1 ribbing.

Row 2 (buttonholes): K1, YO, K2tog, P1, YO, K2tog, K1, YO, K2tog, P1.

BO all sts in patt.

Right Placket

PU 10 sts along right edge of opening.

Work 2 rows in K1, P1 ribbing.

BO all sts in patt.

Hood

You can use straight or circular needles for this step. The width of piece is approx 6½" and can be worked on a short pair of dpns. See page 9 for adapting dpns.

Using straight needles and MC or CC, CO 34 sts.

Work 3 rows in K1, P1 ribbing.

Switch to MC if you started with CC, work in St st until piece measures 1½" from CO.

Next 2 rows: BO 12 sts, work to end.

Work rem 10 sts in St st until piece measures 4" from CO.

BO all sts.

Sew side seams of hood as shown on page 28. Sew hood to neckline, excluding top of placket.

Finishing

Using yarn tails, sew bottom end of placket in place, close holes at leg join, and using mattress st, sew bottom of feet closed. Sew buttons to right placket opposite buttonholes. Weave in yarn tails.

Buttonless Baby Suit

Maybe you know a very small child who would like a little doll but is too young to understand that buttons shouldn't be chewed off. This is the garment to make for that small child's doll. This baby suit is designed to stay on the doll. It has an opening in the back that is laced closed after the garment is placed on the doll. If you choose washable materials, the whole toy can be tossed in the washing machine when necessary. If the doll survives the child's toddlerhood, then you can remove the garment and make the doll a larger wardrobe.

YARNS USED

Suit: Naturally Caron Spa DK in colors Soft Sunshine and Green Sheen.

Doll hair: Bernat Boa in color Raven.

SIZE

Body length: Approx 6½" from shoulder to toes

MATERIALS

Gather supplies for "Basic Baby Suit" in chosen yarn weight. Use washable yarn. In addition, you'll need:

24" of yarn, ribbon, or cord for back laced closure, ⅛" wide

Use contrasting color to knit leaf motif.

LEGS

Instructions are given in fingering-weight yarn; sport- and DK-weight yarn follow in parentheses.

Follow instructions for "Basic Baby Suit" up to point where legs are joined.

BODY

Cont working St st (without making front opening) until piece measures 1¾" from leg join.

DIVIDE FOR FRONTS AND BACK

Place 26 (22, 18) sts on st holder for back of garment. Work 27 (21, 17) rem sts back and forth in St st until front measures 3 (2¾, 2¾)" from leg join, ending with completed WS row.

Next row: K9 (8, 6) sts, BO 9 (5, 5) center front sts, knit to end. Work each side separately.

Right side

Next row (WS): Purl.

Next row: BO 3 (2, 2) sts at neck edge, knit to end.

Next row: Purl. Place rem 6 (5, 4) sts on st holder.

Left side

Join new yarn at outer edge of left shoulder.

Next row: Knit.

Next row: BO 3 (2, 2) sts at neck edge, purl to end.

Next row. Knit. Place rem 6, (5, 4) sts on st holder.

BACK

Divide back sts into 2 sides with 13 (11, 9) sts each. This is beg of back opening and you'll work each side separately.

Right side: Join new yarn at outer edge and work St st until side is even with second row of bound-off sts on front, ending with completed RS row.

Next row: BO 7 (6, 5) sts at neck edge, purl to end. Place rem 6 (5, 4) sts on holder.

Left side: Join yarn at neck edge and work St st until side is even with right side of back, ending with completed WS row.

Next row: BO 7 (6, 5) sts at neck edge, knit to end. Place rem 6 (5, 4) sts on holder.

Turn garment inside out. Work 3-needle BO to join front and back shoulders.

SLEEVES

Work as instructed for "Sleeves" of "Basic Baby Suit" for your chosen yarn weight.

HOOD

Follow instructions for hood of "Basic Baby Suit." Work until hood measures 2". At this point you'll be working on back-center part of hood. Divide rem sts in half and work each side separately. This will form split on back of hood that will align with split on back of garment. Work each side of back of hood until it measures 4". BO all sts.

Sew side seams of hood as shown on page 28. Sew hood to neckline, aligning split in back of hood with split in back of garment. Front edges of hood should be about ¾" apart along front neckline.

LEAF

Follow instructions for your chosen yarn weight.

Fingering-Weight Yarn

CO 3 sts.

Row 1 and odd-numbered rows: Purl.

Row 2: K1, YO, K1, YO, K1–5 sts.

Row 4: K2, YO, K1, YO, K2–7 sts.

Row 6: K3, YO, K1, YO, K3–9 sts.

Row 8: SSK, K5, K2tog–7 sts.

Row 10: SSK, K3, K2tog–5 sts.

Row 12: SSK, K1, K2tog–3 sts.

Row 14: Sl 1-K2tog-psso–1 st. Fasten off.

Sport- and DK-Weight Yarn

CO 3 sts.

Row 1 and odd-numbered rows: Purl.

Row 2: K1, YO, K1, YO, K1–5 sts.

Row 4: K2, YO, K1, YO, K2–7 sts.

Row 6: Ssk, K3, K2tog–5 sts.

Row 8: Ssk, K1, K2tog–3 sts.

Row 10: Sl 1-K2tog-psso–1 st. Fasten off.

All Yarn

Sew leaf to front center of garment and work duplicate st (page 37) over 5 (3, 2) sts to make stem below leaf.

> **Duplicate Stitch**
>
> To make stem, thread green yarn on tapestry needle and bring needle from WS to RS at base of first st to be covered. Insert needle from right to left through top of same st. Bring needle down and insert it at base of same st, bringing it out again at base of st that lies directly above one just covered. Rep for rem duplicate st. Weave in ends.
>
> 

FINISHING

Sew feet and opening at leg join closed. Weave in yarn tails. Place garment on doll and lace back opening closed like a shoelace using yarn, narrow ribbon, or cord. If desired, pull ribbon tails to inside of garment using crochet hook. This may make outfit slightly more childproof.

> **Ribbon Hint**
>
> If you use polyester ribbon, the ends of the ribbon can be very slightly melted to prevent them from raveling. Light a candle and hold the end of the ribbon about half an inch away from the flame briefly, not long enough to discolor the ribbon. After it cools, you should be able to feel a little hard edge on the end of the ribbon. If you accidentally burn it, cut off the end and try again.

Lions and Clown

This lion's mane and clown's wig are made using eyelash yarn for the hood of the Basic Baby Suit. The body of the clown is knit from small scraps of many yarn colors. Alternatively, you could knit the clown body in a solid color and sew small patches to it. Or you could use a self-striping yarn and see what happens. The clown's nose is made from polymer clay and held in place by clear elastic beading cord. You could also use a ½" red round button for the nose.

YARNS USED

Orange Lion

Suit: Knit Picks Palette in colors Golden Heather and Masala.

Mane: Lion Brand Yarn Fun Fur in color Copper.

Doll hair: Crystal Palace Yarns Fizz in color Black.

Clown

Suit: Knit Picks Palette in various colors.

Clown wig: Lion Brand Yarn Fun Fur in color Tangerine.

Doll hair: Crystal Palace Yarns Splash in color Brass.

Brown Lion

Suit: Knit Picks Palette in colors Suede and Brindle Heather.

Mane: Lion Brand Yarn Fun Fur in color Chocolate.

Doll hair: Lion Brand Yarn Fun Fur in color Champagne.

SIZE

Body length: Approx 6½" from shoulder to toes

MATERIALS

Gather supplies for "Basic Baby Suit" in chosen yarn weight. In addition, you'll need:

Approx 6 to 12 yards of eyelash yarn in color of your choice for hood/mane/wig and appropriate-size needles for yarn

½"-diameter round button or small piece of red polymer clay for clown's nose

7" of clear elastic thread or beading cord to attach nose to doll's face

SUIT

Follow hooded "Basic Baby Suit" instructions for your chosen yarn weight up to the hood. Follow instructions (page 40) to make the lion's mane or clown's wig and the lion's tail.

LION'S MANE OR CLOWN'S WIG

Using size 10 needles and eyelash yarn, CO 21 sts.

Work back and forth in garter st (knit every row) for 1½".

Next 2 rows: BO first 7 sts, work to end.

Work rem 7 sts until piece measures 4½" from CO.

BO all sts.

Sew side seams of hood as shown on page 28. Sew hood/mane to neckline of baby suit, but not to top of placket.

LION'S TAIL

(For All Yarn Weights)

Using same yarn as for body, CO 5 (5, 3) sts.

Work I-cord for 4" (page 14).

Join novelty yarn used in hood with MC and work until piece measures 5".

BO all sts.

Weave in yarn tails. Sew tail to back of lion costume.

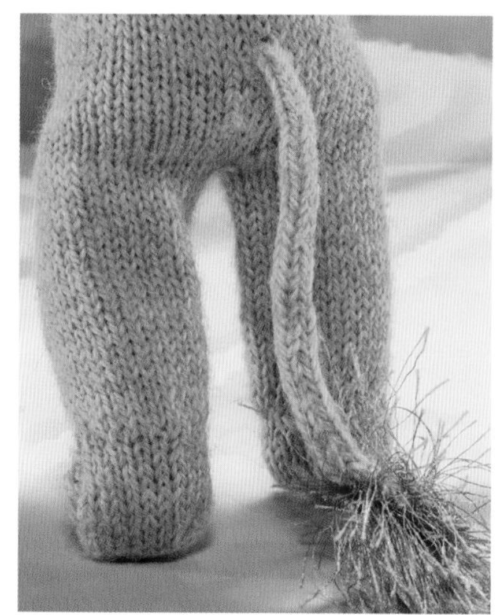

Polymer Clay Nose

Refer to "Making Your Own Buttons" (page 8). Using red polymer clay, roll a ½" or slightly smaller round ball. Slice off about ⅓ of the bead, leaving a flat surface where the portion was removed. Using a tapestry needle, make a hole through the bead, parallel to flattened side. Bake the piece as directed on the clay's package. Thread a 7" length of clear elastic thread or beading cord through the hole and tie the ends together, leaving about ¼" tails after the knot. Place the nose on the face and pull the elastic thread over the head, underneath the hood.

Cats

These cuddly kittens are especially soft and fuzzy when made from luxurious alpaca yarn. The striped cats are knit in one solid color, and then the stripes are added at the end using a duplicate stitch. You can also make a tiger if you use tiger colors.

YARNS USED

Light Gray Cat (page 42)
Suit: Frog Tree Yarns 100% Alpaca Wool Sport Weight in colors 009 (light gray) and 0010 (dark gray).
Doll hair: Lion Brand Yarn Fun Fur in color Black.

Black-and-White Cat (page 42)
Suit: Frog Tree Yarns Alpaca Wool Fingering Weight in colors 100 black and 2310 white.
Doll hair: Bernat Boa in color Soft Mink.

Dark Gray Cat (page 42)
Suit: Frog Tree Yarns Alpaca Wool Sport Weight in colors 0010 (dark gray) and 009 (light gray).
Doll hair: Crystal Palace Yarns Splash in color Espresso.

SIZE

Body length: Approx 6½" from shoulder to toes

MATERIALS

Gather supplies for "Basic Baby Suit" in chosen yarn weight. In addition, you'll need:

Small scrap of pale pink yarn or embroidery floss to add color to the inside of ears (optional)

Set of 5 size 4 (3.5 mm) double-pointed needles for ears if you're using DK-weight yarn

STRIPED CAT

Follow hooded "Basic Baby Suit" instructions for your chosen yarn weight, knitting the entire piece using MC. When the piece is done, use tapestry needle and CC to add stripes with duplicate st. It's easier to do stripes if garment is on doll.

Follow instructions (page 43) to make tail and ears.

BLACK-AND-WHITE CAT

Beg knitting feet of Basic Baby Suit with white yarn. Switch to black yarn after knitting rnd 12 (9, 7). Use white yarn for ribbing on sleeves and hood.

Make ears from black yarn and switch to white yarn after rnd 4 (3, 3).

Follow instructions below to make tail and ears.

TAIL
(FOR ALL YARN WEIGHTS)

CO 5 sts.

Work I-cord (page 14) for 5". If making black-and-white cat, CO with black and work I-cord for 4½", then switch to white and work ½".

Next row: K2tog, K1, K2tog.

Last row: Sl 1-K2tog-psso.

Fasten off last st.

EARS (MAKE 2.)

Follow the instructions for your chosen yarn weight.

Fingering- and Sport-Weight Yarn

Using same size needle as for body, CO 16 sts. Distribute sts on 3 needles and join in rnd.

Rnd 1: Knit.

Rnd 2: Ssk, K6, K2tog, K6–14 sts.

Rnd 3: Knit.

Rnd 4: Ssk, K5, K2tog, K5–12 sts.

Rnd 5: Ssk, K4, K2tog, K4–10 sts.

Rnd 6: Ssk, K3, K2tog, K3–8 sts. It may be easier to knit rem rows using 3 needles instead of 4–1 needle holding sts in front, 1 in back.

Rnd 7: Ssk, K2, K2tog, K2–6 sts.

Rnd 8: Sk2p twice–2 sts. Pass 1 st over other and fasten off.

Using pale pink yarn and tapestry needle, work duplicate st (page 37) over a few sts at base of inner ear.

DK-Weight Yarn

Using size 4 dpns, CO 12 sts. Distribute sts on 3 needles and join in rnd.

Rnd 1: Knit.

Rnd 2: Ssk, K4, K2tog, K4–10 sts.

Rnd 3: Ssk, K3, K2tog, K3–8 sts. It may be easier to knit rem rows using 3 needles instead of 4–1 needle holding sts in front, 1 in back.

Rnd 4: Ssk, K2, K2tog, K2–6 sts.

Rnd 5: Ssk, K1, K2tog, K1–4 sts

Rnd 6: Ssk, K2tog–2 sts. Pass 1 st over other and fasten off.

Using pale pink yarn and tapestry needle, work duplicate st over a few sts at base of inner ear.

FINISHING

Sew ears and tail in place. Weave in yarn tails.

Tiger Cub

With the right colors, you can turn your cat suit into a tiger! Tiger is made from Frog Tree Yarns Alpaca Sport Melange in color 915 (orange). Stripes are made with Frog Tree Yarns Alpaca Wool Fingering Weight in colors 2310 (white) and 100 (black).
Doll hair: Lion Brand Fun Fur in color Chocolate.

Bears

This snuggly bear is one of my favorite outfits. I originally designed the bear using a bulky-weight chenille yarn that was in my stash for untold years. Of course, that yarn is no longer available, but after testing several options, I found that two strands of Knit Picks Crayon held together is a great substitute. Use whatever yarn gives you the correct gauge. Because this suit is made for a larger gauge than the other suits, the directions have been written specifically for this gauge.

YARNS USED

Left Bear

Suit: Two strands of Knit Picks Crayon DK in color Teddy.

Doll hair: Lion Brand Yarn Fun Fur in color Champagne.

Seated Bear

Suit: Two strands of Knit Picks Crayon DK in color Cashew.

Doll hair: Crystal Palace Yarns Splash in color Black.

Right Bear

Suit: One strand of Lion Brand Yarn Wool-Ease in color Mink Brown.

Doll hair: Crystal Palace Yarns Splash in color Woodgrain.

SIZE

Body length: Approx 6½" from shoulder to toes

MATERIALS

This pattern is a complete suit in itself.

Approx 50 g ball of yarn that will knit to gauge of 4 sts to 1". See note at right for using 2 strands from 1 ball.

Set of 5 size 6 and size 8 dpns, 6" or shorter

Size G-4 (4.25 mm) crochet hook

3 buttons, ⅜" to ½" diameter

Tapestry needle

Waste yarn to hold stitches

GAUGE

4 sts = 1" in St st

Using Two Strands of Yarn

If you need to use two strands of yarn to get the required gauge, wind a 50 gram ball into two equal-size balls. Use a strand from each ball.

If using two strands of yarn to achieve gauge, be sure to use two strands for the entire garment, including the ears and tail.

Costume Notes

This costume is longer and narrower than the Basic Baby Suit, and does not exactly match the schematic on page 28, but it fits on the doll just fine. Another difference is that the plackets are knit continuously with the front, not added later. Because of the larger gauge, this is the quickest costume to knit.

RIGHT LEG

Using size 8 dpns, CO 10 sts. Distribute sts on 3 needles and join in rnd.

Rnds 1 and 2: Knit.

Rnd 3: K1, M1, K5, M1, K4–12 sts.

Rnds 4 and 5: Knit.

Rnd 6: K2tog, K4, K2tog, K4–10 sts.

Rnd 7: Knit.

Rnd 8: K3, M1, K3, M1, K3, M1, K1–13 sts.

Cont knitting until leg measures 3¼" from CO.

Next row: Knit first 3 sts of rnd and stop. Keep last 3 sts worked on needle. Place all other sts on waste yarn. Do not cut working yarn.

LEFT LEG

Work as for right leg until piece measures 3¼" from CO.

Next row: Knit incomplete rnd, stopping when 3 sts rem at end of rnd. Leave last 3 sts worked on needle. Place all other sts on waste yarn. Cut working yarn, leaving 10" tail.

JOINING LEGS

Position 2 legs side by side so that last sts worked are to insides of legs. You'll pick up all sts from both legs and distribute them on 4 needles as follows:

Needle 1: PU last st worked on left leg and next 6 sts to be worked on right leg.

Needle 2: PU next 6 sts on right leg.

Needle 3: PU last st on right leg and next 6 sts from inner left leg.

Needle 4: PU rem 6 sts on left leg.

Next row: K2tog, K11, K2tog, K11–24 sts.

Work in St st until piece measures 4¼" from CO. Note there is hole in crotch of joined legs. You'll use yarn tail from left leg to sew hole closed.

BODY

Start row 1 at center front. Work back and forth in St st from this point. The CO sts in rows 1 and 2 will form plackets

Row 1: CO 2 sts at beg of row, purl to end–26 sts.

Row 2: CO 2 sts at beg of row, knit to end–28 sts.

Row 3: Purl.

Row 4 (buttonhole row): K1, K2tog, YO, knit to end.

Row 5: Purl.

Row 6: Knit.

Row 7: Purl.

Row 8: Rep row 4.

Row 9: Purl.

Row 10: Knit.

Divide sts for fronts and back on 3 needles as follows: Left front, 8 sts; back, 12 sts; right front, 8 sts. Cont working on left front.

LEFT FRONT

Row 1: Purl.

Row 2 (buttonhole row): K1, K2tog, YO, knit to end.

Row 3: Purl.

Row 4: Knit.

Row 5: BO 2 sts at neck edge, purl to end—6 sts.

Row 6: Knit.

Row 7: BO 2 sts at neck edge, purl to end—4 sts.

Place rem 4 sts on holder for shoulder.

RIGHT FRONT

Join yarn at right arm opening.

Row 1: Purl.

Row 2: Knit.

Row 3: Purl.

Row 4: BO 2 sts at neck edge, knit to end—6 sts.

Row 5: Purl.

Row 6: BO 2 sts at neck edge, knit to end—4 sts.

Row 7: Knit.

Place rem 4 sts on holder for shoulder.

BACK

With RS facing you, join new yarn at side and work in St st until even with front shoulder.

Next row: Work first 4 sts, BO next 4 sts, work to end.

SHOULDER SEAMS

Turn garment inside out. Place shoulder sts back on needle. Join front and back shoulders using 3-needle BO (page 11). Turn garment RS out.

SLEEVES

Using crochet hook for pickup (page 12), PU 12 sts around armhole. Distribute sts on 3 dpns.

Knit in rnd in St st for approx 1½".

Next rnd: Work K1, P1 ribbing.

BO in ribbing patt.

HOOD

CO 22 sts.

Work 2 rows in K1, P1 ribbing.

Work in St st until piece measures 1½" from CO.

Next 2 rows: BO first 7 sts, work to end.

Work rem sts in St st until hood measures 4" from CO.

BO all sts.

Sew side seams of hood as shown on page 28.

Sew hood to neckline but do not sew it to top of plackets.

EARS (MAKE 2.)

Using size 6 dpns, CO 9 sts. Distribute sts on 3 dpns and join in rnd.

Rnd 1: Knit.

Rnd 2: *K2tog, K1; rep from * to end of rnd—6 sts.

Rnd 3: Knit.

Cut yarn, thread tapestry needle and pull yarn through rem sts. Fasten off.

TAIL

Make bobble as follows.

Using size 6 dpns, CO 1 st. Knit in front, back, front, back, front of next st, making 5 sts out of 1.

Work in St st for 4 rows.

Next row: From left to right, lift second, third, fourth, and fifth sts over first st. Fasten off.

Thread tapestry needle with yarn tail and pull yarn through some of the edge sts all around circumference of bobble. Draw this yarn tight, making bobble into a little ball.

FINISHING

Sew feet closed. Sew bases of plackets to secure them. Sew 3 buttons to right placket.

Sew hole in crotch closed. Weave in yarn tails. Sew ears and tail in place. It's easier to sew them in place if you put the garment on doll first.

Rabbits

Who knew you could knit rabbit ears? The upright ears on the white rabbit are supported by ear-shaped forms made from stiff felt—a little feat of crafty engineering. If you're feeling less ambitious, you can always make floppy ears.

YARNS USED

White Rabbit (page 50)
Suit: Frog Tree Yarns 100% Alpaca Wool Fingering Weight in colors 2310 (white) and 95.
Doll hair: Crystal Palace Yarns Splash in color Black.

Gray Rabbit (page 50)
Suit: Frog Tree Yarns Alpaca Wool Sport Weight in color 009.
Rabbit ears: Frog Tree Yarns Alpaca Wool Fingering Weight in color 95.
Doll hair: Lion Brand Fun Fur in color Champagne.

SIZE

Body length: Approx 6½" from shoulder to toes

MATERIALS

Gather supplies for "Basic Baby Suit" in chosen yarn weight. In addition, you'll need:

4 yds of pink yarn for feet, sleeve ribbing, and insides of ears

For sport and DK weight, you'll need size 4 dpns for ears

For rabbit with upright ears:

1 piece of stiff felt in similar color to rabbit, 6" x 6" (available at craft stores); OR you may use heavy-weight interfacing instead

Sewing needle and thread in color to match rabbit

Thimble (optional)

BODY

Instructions are given in fingering-weight yarn; sport- and DK-weight yarn follow in parentheses.

Following "Basic Baby Suit" instructions for your chosen yarn weight, CO with pink yarn and knit first 2 (1, 1) rnds in pink. Then switch to MC and cont instructions for suit, including hood. Make sleeve ribbing pink. When you switch to pink on sleeves, knit 1 row in pink before starting ribbing.

FLOPPY EARS (MAKE 2.)

Follow instructions for your chosen yarn weight.

Fingering-Weight Yarn

With same size needles as body, CO 16 sts. Distribute sts on 3 dpns and join in rnd.

Knit until piece measures ¾" from CO.

Inc rnd: (M1, K8) twice–18 sts.

Knit until piece measures 1" from CO.

Inc rnd: (M1, K9) twice–20 sts.

Knit until piece measures 2½" from CO.

Dec rnd: (Ssk, K8) twice–18 sts.

Next 2 rnds: Knit.

Dec rnd: (Ssk, K7) twice–16 sts.

Knit until piece measures 3¼" from CO.

Dec rnd: K2tog 8 times–8 sts.

Next rnd: Knit.

Dec rnd: K2tog 4 times–4 sts.

Thread tapestry needle with yarn tail and pull yarn through rem sts. Fasten off. Sew ears in place.

Sport- or DK-Weight Yarn

Instructions are given in sport-weight yarn; DK-weight yarn follows in parentheses. Note that size 4 dpns are used for sport or DK.

Using size 4 dpns, CO 14 (12) sts and join in rnd.

Knit until piece measures ¾" from CO.

Inc rnd: [M1, K7 (6)] twice–16 (14) sts.

Knit until piece measures 2½" from CO.

Dec rnd: [Ssk, K6 (5)] twice–14 (12) sts.

Knit until piece measures 3¼" from CO.

Dec rnd: K2tog 7 (6) times–7 (6) sts.

Next rnd: Knit.

Thread tapestry needle with yarn tail and pull yarn through rem sts. Fasten off. Sew ears in place.

UPRIGHT EARS

To make ears stand up, you'll sew a small piece of stiff felt inside top of hood. Ear forms are sewn in place on outside of hood, supported by felt inside hood. Then knit ears are placed over ear forms and sewn in place. To keep ears upright, start by making ear forms; then follow knitting instructions to make ear covers. Make 2 of each.

Ear Forms

Use pattern (page 53) to cut 4 ears out of stiff felt and bend each one at fold line. With flaps going in opposite directions as shown, baste 2 shapes together to form ear. Make 2 ear forms.

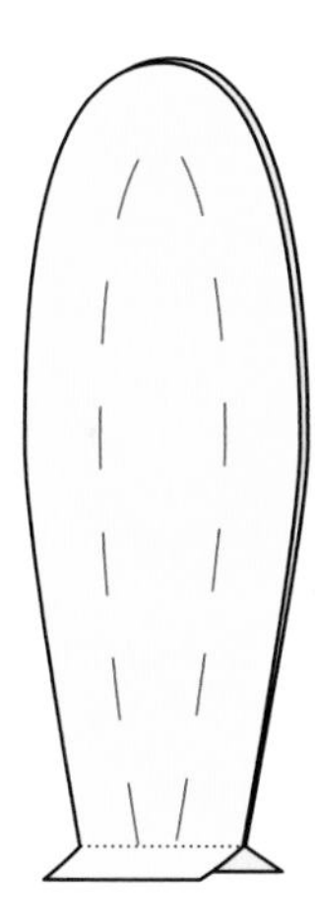

Cut a 1" x 1¾" piece of stiff felt and slightly round the corners. Place this piece inside top of hood with longer side going across and shorter side going from front to back. Align front edge of felt where knit hood changes from ribbing to St st. Sew this piece in place.

Position flaps of ear forms on outside of hood and sew them on through the layers of the knit hood and inside piece of stiff felt. A thimble really helps to push needle through felt when sewing these layers.

Knitting Ears

The ears have flaps on front and back at base of ear. These flaps cover base of ear forms. Knitting instructions for ears begin with knitting these little flaps. Instructions are given in fingering-weight yarn; sport/DK-weight yarn follows in parentheses. Make 2. Use size 4 dpns for sport or DK weight.

Using MC, CO 6 (5) sts. Work 4 (3) rows in St st. This is 1 of the 2 flaps for base of ear. Rep instructions for second flap.

Place both flaps side by side on 1 needle, with RS facing same way. Knit across all sts of flaps to join them. Distribute these sts on 3 needles and join in rnd.

Knit until piece measures 3" from CO.

Next rnd: K2tog 6 (5) times–6 (5) sts.

Fasten off. Thread tapestry needle with yarn tail and pull through rem sts. Weave in ends. Make two.

Using pink yarn and tapestry needle, duplicate st (page 37) inner ear to create what looks like inside of rabbit ears.

Duplicate stitch

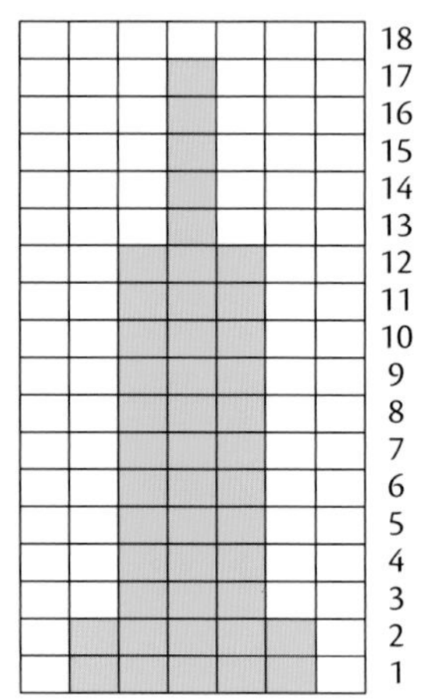

Slide knit ears over ear forms and spread flaps on top of hood over flaps of stiff felt. Using yarn tails from knit flaps, sew knit flaps to hood of garment, completely covering felt.

FINISHING

Weave in yarn tails. Make pom-pom for tail and sew in place.

Pom-Poms

Pom-poms are easy and fun to make.

1. Cut 2 circles from cardboard, 1¼" in diameter. Cut a hole in the center of each circle, about ½" in diameter. Thread a long piece of yarn through a tapestry needle. Hold the two circles together, insert the needle into the hole, wrap it around, and then back through the hole. Repeat, working evenly around the circle, rethreading the needle when necessary until the circle is filled completely. When you think you have it full enough, add some more. The fuller, the better!

2. Use sharp scissors to cut the yarn around the edge between the two pieces of cardboard.

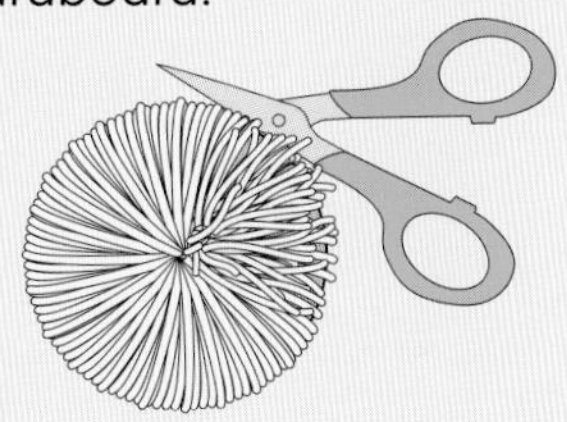

3. Cut a 12"-long piece of yarn. Run this yarn between the two circles and tie it very tightly. Slide the circles off the pom-pom and fluff it out. Trim any stray ends.

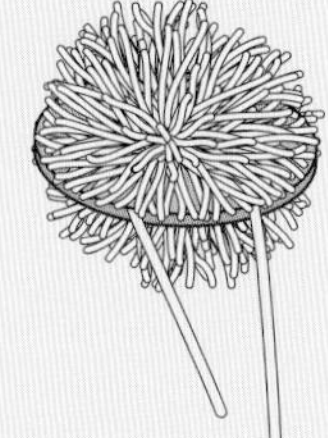

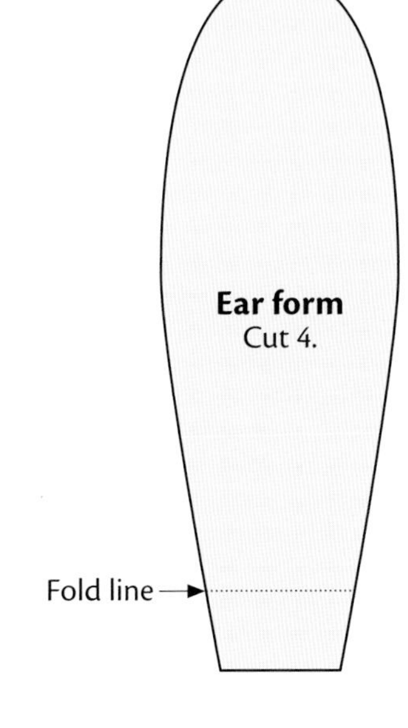

Squirrels

If you have never knit a squirrel costume before, you probably don't realize how challenging it can be to find squirrel-colored yarn (a knitting dilemma if there ever was one). I researched squirrels online and found that some squirrels are entirely black and some are entirely white. (*There's* an easy solution to the yarn dilemma!) The squirrels around my house in northern Colorado are rusty red fox squirrels. The gray squirrel is common in the eastern United States. As I was working on the squirrel project, my children spent two weeks in Pennsylvania with their cousins, where squirrels are gray. So I made a pair of squirrel cousins, East and West.

YARNS USED

Brown Squirrel

Suit: Shirakaba from Noro in color 7.

Tail: Crystal Palace Yarns Splash in color Brass.

Doll hair: Crystal Palace Yarns Splash in color Black.

Gray Squirrel

Suit: Dale of Norway Falk Dalegarm in color 3841.

Tail: Crystal Palace Yarns Splash in color Mink.

Doll hair: Lion Brand Yarn Fun Fur in color Chocolate.

SIZE

Body length: Approx 6½" from shoulder to toes

MATERIALS

Gather supplies for "Basic Baby Suit" in chosen yarn weight. In addition, you'll need:

Partial skein of novelty yarn, such as Crystal Palace Yarns Splash, for squirrel tail

Size 10 (6 mm) straight needles for tail

Small piece (about 4" x 4") of felt or fleece fabric for ears, in coordinating color

12"-long chenille stem, any color (it will not show; available at craft stores)

BODY

Follow hooded "Basic Baby Suit" instructions for your chosen yarn weight. Then follow instructions (page 56) to make tail and ears.

Using Self-Striping Yarn

The Shirakaba yarn used for the brown squirrel is a self-striping silk blend, perfectly squirrel colored. I started the first foot at a place where the stripe was gold and knit up the leg. For the second leg, I unwound the ball to a similar place in the stripe sequence where I had started the first leg, cut the yarn at that place, and started the second foot. This resulted in two similar-colored legs. For the rest of the squirrel I just let the stripes unfold as they were, and it turned out wonderfully.

TAIL

This piece uses a short-row technique (page 13). If you use a novelty yarn other than Splash, refer to instructions for skunk tail (page 60), which will work better. Just leave out color changes indicated for skunk.

Using size 10 needles and 1 strand of body yarn and 1 strand of Splash held tog, CO 16 sts. (If you're using fingering-weight yarn, use 2 strands held tog with 1 strand of Splash.)

Row 1: K16.

Row 2: P16.

Row 3: K11, turn work, leave rem sts unworked.

Row 4: P11.

Rows 5–12: Rep rows 1–4 twice.

Row 13: K16.

Row 14: P16.

BO all sts. Fasten off, leaving a long tail for sewing.

Fold piece in half lengthwise, whichever side you like to the outside. Sew short end and long side closed. Bend chenille stem as shown below and insert narrow end all the way into tail. Sew other end of tail closed and sew tail to costume on back, about 1" from leg join. Bend tail into shape.

EARS

Cut 2 ears out of chosen material using ear pattern below. Fold ears in half lengthwise and put a st in bottom of each ear to hold fold in place. Sew ears in place on hood.

Get out some nuts.

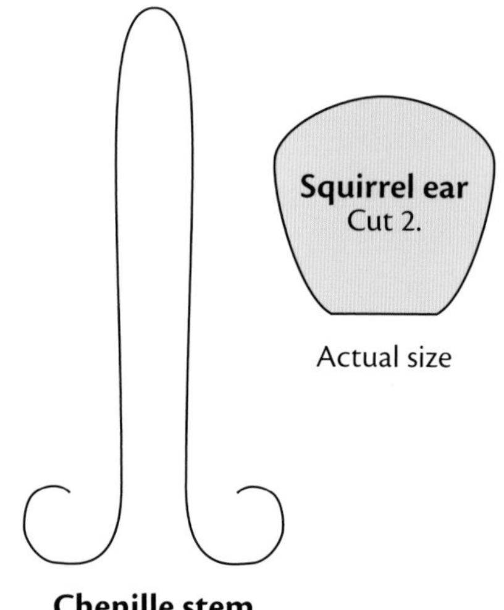

Chenille stem
Smaller than actual size

Skunk

My adolescent daughter tells me that her friends' mothers don't spend their time knitting miniature skunk costumes. I don't doubt that. But I'm not the only one who has ever thought of a little skunk costume. In the animated Disney classic Peter Pan, one of the Lost Boys wears one. So this pattern is either a skunk costume or a Lost Boy outfit.

YARNS USED

Suit: Knit Picks Merino Style DK in color Coal.

Tail: Knit Picks Merino Style DK in color black, Knit Picks Swish DK in color white, and Lion Brand Yarn Fun Fur in colors white and black.

Doll hair: Bernat Boa in color Soft Mink.

SIZE

Body length: Approx 6½" from shoulder to toes

MATERIALS

Gather supplies for "Basic Baby Suit" in chosen yarn weight. In addition, you'll need:

Small amount of body yarn in black and white for tail

Partial skeins of Lion Brand Yarn Fun Fur in black and white for tail

Size 8 (5 mm) straight needles for tail

A small piece (2" x 8") of white felt or fleece for skunk's stripe

12"-long chenille stem, any color (it will not show)

Small piece of black felt or fleece for ears

BODY

Follow hooded "Basic Baby Suit" instructions for your chosen yarn weight, making the garment all black and using black buttons. Then follow instructions below to make the white stripe and tail.

WHITE STRIPE

Using the pattern (page 60), cut 1 piece from the white felt or fleece. Fold the narrow end ½" over front of hood. Starting at fold, sew stripe on hood and down back with a length of black yarn using a backstitch. Sts used to sew stripe will create a narrow black stripe near each side of white piece.

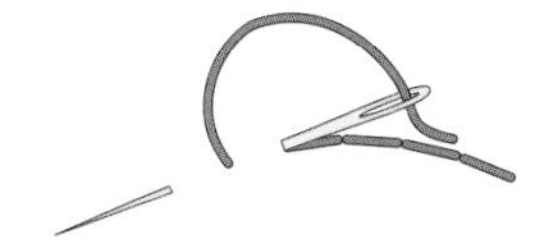

Backstitch

TAIL

This piece uses a short-row technique (page 13).

Use size 8 needles (straight or circular) and 1 strand of body yarn and 1 strand of Fun Fur yarn held tog. (If you're using fingering-weight yarn, use 2 strands of it held tog with 1 strand of Fun Fur yarn.)

Starting with white yarns, CO 23 sts.

Row 1: K23.

Switch to black yarns.

Row 2: P23.

Row 3: K23.

Switch to white yarns.

Row 4: P23.

Row 5: K14, turn work, leave rem sts unworked.

Row 6: P14.

Row 7: K23.

Switch to black yarn. The rest of the piece is worked in black, and will be underside of tail.

Row 8: P23.

Row 9: K23.

Switch to white yarns.

Row 10: P23.

Row 11: K23.

Switch to black yarns.

Row 12: P23.

Row 13: K23.

Row 14: P23.

Row 15: K23.

Row 16: P23.

Row 17: K14, turn work, leave rem sts unworked.

Row 18: P14.

Row 19: K23.

Row 20: P23.

Row 21: K23.

BO all sts. Fasten off, leaving a long tail for sewing. Fold the piece in half lengthwise, knitted sts to outside. Sew short end and long side closed. Bend chenille stem as shown on page 56 and insert narrow end all the way into tail. Sew other end of tail closed. With white stripe facing toward body, sew tail to back of costume about 1" from leg join. Bend tail into shape. Plug your nose.

EARS

Cut 2 ears from black felt or fleece using pattern at right. Sew in place on hood of skunk costume.

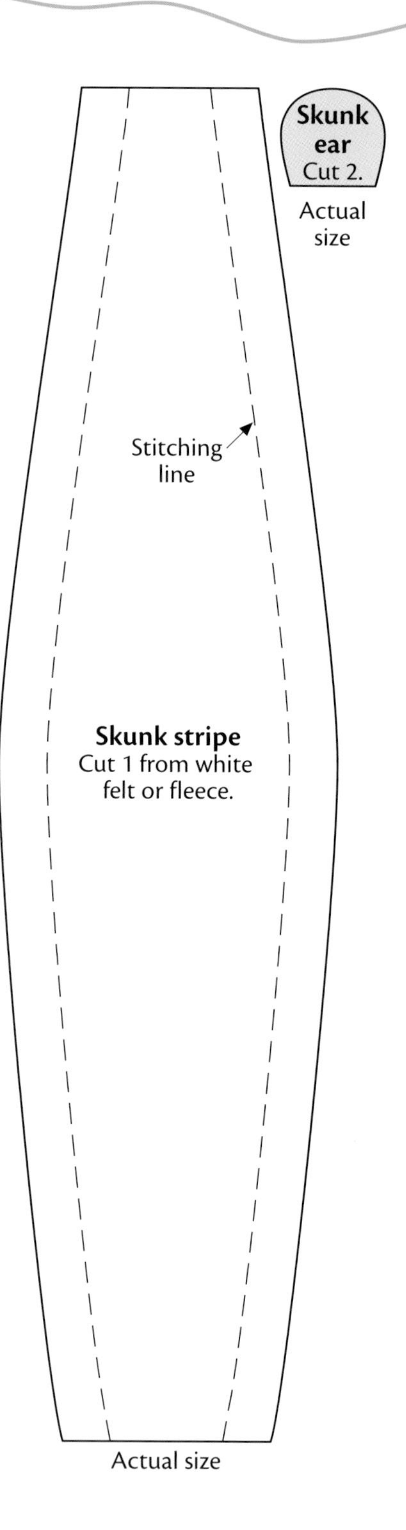

Piglet

Sometimes knitting gives us exactly what we need, like a corkscrew stitch that makes a perfect pig's tail.

YARNS USED

Left Piglet

Suit: Knit Picks Yarn Simply Cotton Sport Weight in color Dogwood Heather.

Doll hair: Crystal Palace Yarns Splash in color Black.

Right Piglet

Suit: Naturally Caron Spa DK in color Rose Bisque.

Doll hair: Patons Allure in color Ebony.

Seated Piglet

Suit: Frog Tree Yarns Alpaca Wool Fingering Weight in colors 95 (pink) and 2310 (white).

Doll hair: Lion Brand Yarn Fun Fur in color Champagne.

SIZE

Body length: Approx 6½" from shoulder to toes

MATERIALS

Gather supplies for "Basic Baby Suit" in chosen yarn weight. In addition, you'll need:

6" x 6" square of pink felt or fleece for ears

Sewing needle and thread to match felt

Small piece of pink polymer clay (about ½" diameter ball) for nose

Approx 7" of clear elastic thread or beading cord to attach nose to doll's face

BODY

Follow hooded "Basic Baby Suit" instructions for your chosen yarn weight. Then follow instructions to make tail, ears, and snout.

CORKSCREW TAIL (FOR ALL YARN WEIGHTS)

CO 8 (8, 12) sts very loosely.

Row 1: K1f&b in each st across row—16 (16, 24) sts.

Row 2: BO purlwise.

Fasten off last st. Twist piece into corkscrew shape. Sew tail into place, approx 1" above leg divide. Weave in yarn tails.

EARS (MAKE 2.)

Cut two ears from fleece or felt using pattern below. Make crease in ear by folding in half from bottom to top. Place st in base of ear approx ¼" from crease to hold crease in place. Open ear and position as desired; sew in place.

SNOUT

Refer to "Making Your Own Buttons" (page 8) for working with polymer clay. Using ball of pink polymer clay about ½" diameter, form cylinder that's ⅜" diameter and ½" high. Use tapestry needle to poke 2 holes in one end of cylinder for nostrils. Then make hole from side to side through back end of cylinder. This is hole you'll pass cord through to hold snout in place on doll's face. Bake snout as directed on clay's package. Thread 7" length of clear elastic thread or beading cord through hole and tie ends together, leaving about ¼" tails after knot. Put snout on your doll and find a pigpen.

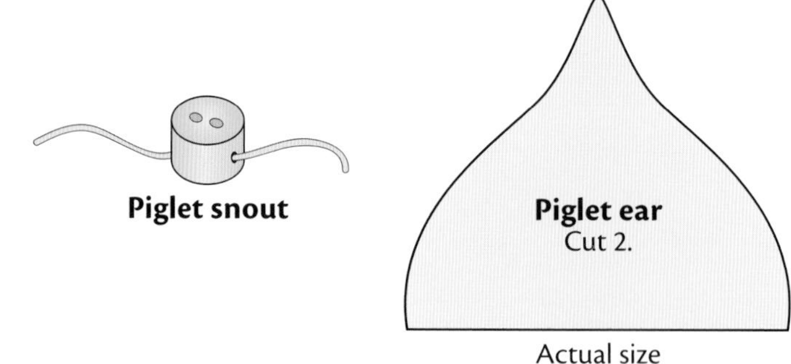

Lacy Dress

I first envisioned this little dress after seeing a bright red cotton dress my mother knit for one of her small granddaughters. I thought I would make a similar dress, only much smaller. I ended up knitting, tearing out, knitting again, and tearing out, as sometimes happens. Though I am happy with the final design, it looks nothing like the inspiration piece, which also sometimes happens.

YARNS USED

Dress and tights: Frog Tree Yarns Alpaca Wool Fingering Weight in colors 28 (rose), 2310 (white), and 100 (black).
Doll hair: Crystal Palace Yarns Fizz in color Black.

SIZE

Dress: Approx 4½" long

Tights: Approx 5¼" long

MATERIALS

Note that this project is for fingering-weight yarn only.

Partial skein of fingering-weight yarn in color rose for dress

Partial skein of fingering-weight yarn in color white for tights and collar

Partial skein of fingering-weight yarn in color black for shoes

Size 2 (2.75 mm) straight or circular needles

Set of 5 size 2 (2.75 mm) double-pointed needles, 5" or 6" long

4 very small stitch holders or small safety pins

Waste yarn to hold stitches

2 stitch markers

2 seed beads for earrings

GAUGE

8 sts = 1" in St st

Design Notes

This frilly dress was designed using Elizabeth Zimmerman's percentage formula for knitting a seamless sweater. It's worked from the bottom up. The edges of the sleeves and the lower edge of the dress are knit on straight needles first, and then joined into a circle and worked in the round. The body is worked in one piece to the underarm, and then the sleeves are worked and joined to the body. The yoke is then worked, completing the front, back, and sleeves together. The underarm seams are closed using the Kitchener stitch. If you've never made a sweater in this manner, this will be good practice for a larger garment.

DRESS

Body

Front and back of dress are identical.

Using rose yarn and straight or circular needle, CO 113 sts.

Row 1 (RS): Knit.

Row 2: K2, *K1, sl this st back on LH needle, lift next 8 sts on LH needle over this st and off needle, YO twice, knit first st again, K2; rep from * to end.

Row 3: K1, *P2tog, drop 1 loop of 2 yarn overs made in previous row and (K1, K1tbl) twice in the rem loop, P1, rep from * to last st, K1.

Rows 4–6: Knit.

After working these rows, there should be 10 scallops and 62 sts.

Distribute sts on 4 dpns, pm at beg of rnd and between st 31 and 32 (in middle of rnd). Join for knitting in the rnd.

Rnds 1–5: Knit.

Rnd 6: K2tog, knit to next marker, K2tog, knit to end of rnd.

Rep rnds 1–6 a total of 4 times—54 sts.

Next rnd: K2 sts into next rnd; this will place working yarn between an underarm and the front.

Place all sts on 4 separate holders as follows: 23 sts for front, 4 sts for underarm, 23 sts for back, and 4 sts for underarm. Use small safety pins for st holders on the underarms and waste yarn to hold the sts for front and back.

Sleeves

First 6 rows are knit back and forth, and then joined in rnd.

Using straight needles and rose yarn, CO 23 sts.

Row 1: Knit.

Row 2: Purl.

Row 3: K3, (M1, K1) 3 times, (P2tog) 6 times, (M1, K1) twice, M1, K3.

Row 4: Purl.

Rows 5 and 6: Knit.

Distribute sts on 3 dpns and join in rnd.

Rnds 7–11: Knit.

K2 and stop, place last 4 sts worked on very small holder. Place rem sts on waste yarn.

Rep for second sleeve.

Joining Sleeves to Body

The sets of 4 sts on very small holders from sleeves and body will become underarm seams, and will be joined later using Kitchener st.

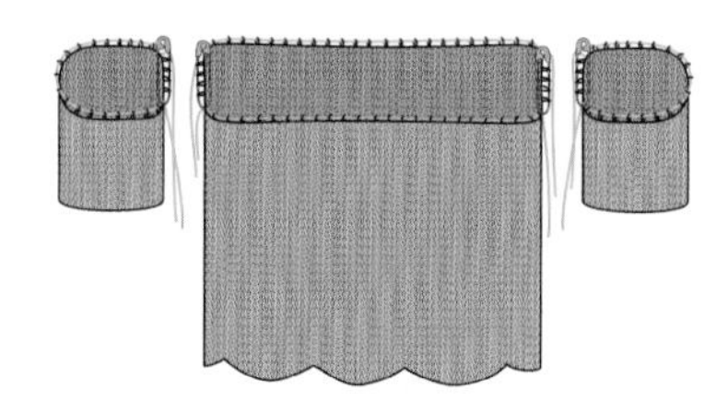

Pick up rem sts from front, back, and sleeves held on waste yarn and distribute them on 4 dpns—84 sts. The underarm sts will stay on their holders for now.

Rnd 1: *P2, P2tog; rep from * to end of rnd—63 sts.

Rnd 2: Knit.

Rnd 3: Purl.

Rnd 4: *K2, K2tog; rep from * to last 3 sts, K3—48 sts.

Lace Yoke

Knit 1 complete rnd. Knit partial rnd until you get to midpoint of a sleeve. Stop and pm. This will be beg of all other rnds.

Rnd 1: K3, *YO, sl 1-K1-psso, K6, rep from * to last 3 sts, K3.

Rnd 2: Knit.

Rnd 3: K3, *K2tog, YO, K1, YO, sl 1-K1-psso, K3, rep from * to last 2 sts, K2.

Rnd 4: Knit.

Rnd 5: Rep rnd 1.

Rnds 6 and 7: Knit.

Rnd 8: *K1, K2tog, rep from * to end of rnd—32 sts.

Change to white yarn.

Rnds 9 and 10: Knit.

The fancy collar of this dress is a picot bind off. BO 2 sts, *sl st back on LH needle, use cable CO (see box at right) to CO 2 sts, then BO 4 sts, rep from * to end. Fasten off last st.

Cable Cast On

1. Insert tip of RH needle between next 2 sts on LH needle.
2. Wrap yarn around and draw loop through space between 2 sts.
3. Insert LH needle into this loop from right to left and remove RH needle from loop. You've just cast on 1 st that is now the first st on LH needle. Repeat these 3 steps for each st.

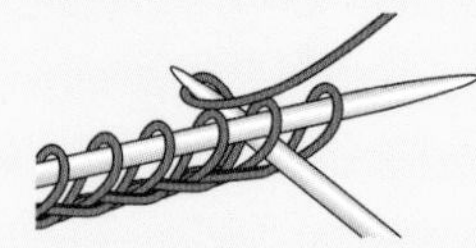

Insert needle between 2 stitches. Knit a stitch.

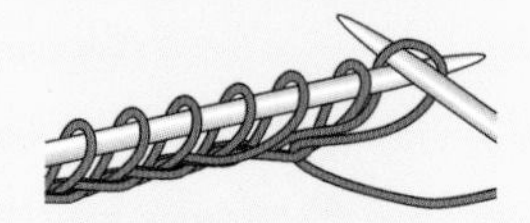

Place new stitch on left needle.

Finishing

Using yarn tails, sew seams of lower edges of body and sleeves tog. Place underarm sts from sleeve on one needle and underarm sts from body on another needle. Close underarm seam with Kitchener st (page 14). Rep for second underarm seam. Weave in yarn tails.

TIGHTS AND SHOES

Using dpns and white yarn, CO 40 sts. Distribute sts on 3 dpns and join in rnd.

Work 3 rnds in K1, P1 ribbing.

Work in St st until piece measures 2" from CO.

Divide for legs: K20 sts and place rem 20 sts on waste yarn.

First Leg

Distribute first 20 sts on 3 needles. On third needle, CO 2 sts. These 2 sts will be at crotch of legs. Join the 22 sts in rnd and knit until leg measures 2½" from leg divide.

Next rnd: *K5, K2tog; rep from * twice, end K1–19 sts.

Switch to black yarn if making tights with shoes, or cont with white yarn if making ballet slippers shown with "Ballerina" (page 70).

Arrange sts so that needle 1 has 7 sts, needle 2 has 5 sts, and needle 3 has 7 sts. Arrange needles so that intersection of needles 1 and 3 is heel. Needle 2 sts are for toe.

Shoes

Use M1 for all increases.

Cont with black yarn for tights with shoes or white yarn for tights with ballet slippers.

Rnd 1: K1, M1, K17, M1, K1–21 sts.

Rnd 2: Knit.

(For ballet slippers, switch to pink yarn.)

Rnd 3: K10, M1, K1, M1, K10–23 sts.

Rnd 4: K10, M1, K3, M1, K10–25 sts.

Rnd 5: K10, M1, K5, M1, K10–27 sts.

Rnd 6: K10, ssk, K3, K2tog, K10–25 sts.

Rnd 7: K10, ssk, K1, K2tog, K10–23 sts.

Rnd 8: K10, sl 1-K2tog-psso, K10–21 sts.

Rnd 9: K1, K2tog, K7, K2tog, K6, K2tog, K1–18 sts.

Rnd 10: K1, K2tog, K3, K2tog, K2, K2tog, K3, K2tog, K1–14 sts.

Divide sts on 2 needles and close shoe or slipper with Kitchener st.

Second Leg

Distribute 20 sts for second leg on 3 needles and knit them. At end of 20 sts, use crochet hook and working yarn to PU 2 sts from other leg, where 2 sts were CO at crotch of first leg. Join in rnd and knit until leg measures 2½" from leg divide. Make second shoe as for first.

Finishing

Weave in yarn tails.

Ballerina

This dress was inspired by the Layered Ruffle stitch pattern in Nicky Epstein's book *Knitting on the Edge.* While the book is a stitch dictionary of knitted edgings, I saw in it the dress of a ballerina.

YARNS USED

Dress: Frog Tree Yarns Alpaca Wool Fingering Weight in colors 95 (pink) and 2310 (white).
Doll hair: Patons Allure in color Mink.

SIZE

Dress: Approx 4½" long

MATERIALS

Note that this project is for fingering-weight yarn only.

Partial skein of fingering-weight yarn in color pink for dress and ballet slippers

Partial skein of fingering-weight yarn in color white for tights

Set of 5 size 2 (2.75 mm) double-pointed needles

Size 15 (10 mm) straight needles for hair bobble

Size E-4 (3.5 mm) crochet hook

Waste yarn to hold stitches

Tapestry needle

1 yard of 1⁄16"-wide pink satin ribbon for ties on ballet slippers

½ yard of ¼"-wide pink satin ribbon for hair bow

GAUGE

8 sts = 1" in St st

BALLET DRESS

Bottom Tutu

With pink, CO 81 sts. Distribute sts on 3 dpns and join in rnd. Make join so that bumpy side of CO faces out (RS).

Rnd 1: Knit.

Rnd 2: Purl.

Rnd 3: Knit.

Work in St st (knit every rnd) until piece measures 2¼" from CO.

Next rnd: *K1, K3tog; rep from * to last st, K1—41 sts.

Place sts on waste yarn to hold.

K3tog Hint

When working K3tog, give yarn a little extra tug to snug up those 3 sts, so completed sts on RH needle are as evenly spaced as possible.

Top Tutu

Work as for bottom skirt, except work until piece measures only 1⅝" from CO.

Next rnd: *K1, K3tog; rep from * to last st, K1—41 sts.

Leave this layer on needles.

Joining Layers of Tutu

Place 7 sts from bottom tutu on their own needle. Place bottom layer inside top layer with inside sts parallel with next sts to be worked of outer layer.

Join two layers with 3-needle join. This is similar to 3-needle BO (page 11), except that you won't bind off sts but rather leave them on RH needle. When you have worked all sts that you picked up from bottom layer, PU 7 more sts on bottom layer and work 3-needle join as with next sts on top layer. Cont in this manner until all sts are joined—41 sts.

Next rnd: Purl.

Next rnd: Knit.

Work in St st (knit every rnd) until piece measures ⅝" above purl row at waistline.

Divide sts for front (21 sts) and back (20 sts). Front and back will be worked separately in St st.

Bodice Front

Work back and forth in St st until piece measures 1⅝" above purl row at waistline; end with WS row.

Next RS row: K8, BO center 5 sts, knit to end.

Work each shoulder separately, starting with side where yarn is still attached.

***Row 1:** Work to neck edge.

Row 2: BO 2 sts at neck edge, work to end—6 sts.

Row 3: Work to neck edge.

Row 4: BO 1 st at neck edge, work to end—5 sts.

Row 5: Work to neck edge.

Place rem 5 sts on holder.*

Join new yarn to outer edge of other shoulder. Rep from * to *.

Bodice Back

Put back sts from holder onto needle. With RS facing you, join new yarn at side of back. Work back and forth in St st until piece measures 2" from purl row above waistline; end with WS row.

Next RS row: K7, BO center 6 sts, knit to end.

Work shoulders of back separately, starting with side where yarn is still attached.

***Row 1:** Work to neck edge.

Row 2: BO 2 sts at neck edge, work to end—5 sts.

Row 3: Work to neck edge.

Place rem 5 sts on holder.*

Join new yarn to outer edge of other shoulder. Rep from * to *.

Put shoulder sts back on needle and use 3-needle BO to join front and back shoulders.

Sleeves

Using crochet hook for pickup (page 12), PU 29 sts around armhole opening. Distribute sts on 3 dpns.

Knit in rnd in St st until sleeve measures 1".

Next rnd: *K3, K2tog; rep from * to last 4 sts, K2, K2tog–23 sts.

Next rnd: Purl.

BO all sts kw. Fasten off.

Finishing

Work 1 rnd of sc around neckline, starting and ending at a shoulder seam.

Weave in yarn tails.

Block dress to keep edges from curling.

TIGHTS WITH BALLET SLIPPERS

Follow instructions given for "Tights and Shoes" (page 69), noting instructions specific to ballet slippers.

Cut 1/16"-wide ribbon into 4 pieces, 9" long, and singe ends as directed in hint box (page 37). Place end of a ribbon on each side top edge of ballet slipper, approx 1/4" forward of center-back heel. Angle ribbons toward front and sew in place. Wrap ribbons around lower leg 3 times and tie bow in back as shown.

BALLERINA HAIRDO

This doll's hair was made from Patons Allure. If you use a different yarn, you'll have to experiment with needle size.

Actual size

To make an elegant ballerina hairstyle, knit or crochet hair and sew in place as instructed (page 21). Make bobble as follows.

Large Bobble

Using same yarn as hair and size 15 needle, CO 1 st.

Row 1: Knit into front and back of the st 3 times, then knit the st–7 sts.

Row 2: Purl.

Row 3: Knit.

Row 4: P2tog 3 times, K1–4 sts.

Row 5: K2tog twice–2 sts.

Pass 1 st over other. Fasten off, leaving 12" tail. Thread tapestry needle using yarn tail and draw yarn through some of edge sts all around circumference of bobble. Place wad of yarn in center of bobble. Draw yarn tight, making bobble into little ball. Sew bobble in place on doll's head. Tie length of 1/4"-wide ribbon around bobble. Put on some classical music.

Skater Dude

Maybe your doll is the skater type. Make him some long shorts (or short pants), a T-shirt, and some skater-looking shoes. Of course, these designs can be varied for the non-skater types too.

YARNS USED

Skater outfit: Knit Picks Palette in colors Golden Heather, Blue Note Heather, Black, and White.
Doll hair: Lion Brand Yarn Fun Fur in Black.

SIZE

Body length: Approx 6½" from shoulder to toes

MATERIALS

Note that this project is for fingering-weight yarn only.

Partial skein of fingering-weight yarn in color gold for T-shirt

Partial skein of fingering-weight yarn in color blue for pants

Small amounts of fingering-weight yarn in color black for shoes

Set of 5 size 2 (2.75 mm) double-pointed needles, 5" or 6" long

2 small stitch holders

2 stitch markers

Waste yarn for holding stitches

Size E-4 (3.5 mm) crochet hook

Tapestry needle

Embroidery floss for shoelaces (optional)

GAUGE

8 sts = 1"

SHIRT

Using gold yarn, CO 50 sts. Distribute sts on 3 dpns and join in rnd.

Work 4 rnds in K1, P1 ribbing. On last rnd, pm at beg of rnd and in middle of rnd (between 25th and 26th sts).

Rnd 1: Knit.

Rnd 2: K2tog, knit to next marker, K2tog, knit to end of rnd.

Rep rnds 1 and 2 another 4 times—40 sts.

Knit 1 more rnd.

Divide for front and back. Keeping decs on sides of garment, place 20 sts on 1 needle for front and other 20 sts on another needle for back.

Front

Work back and forth in St st until piece measures 2" from CO, ending with WS row.

Next RS row: K8, BO 4 sts, knit to end.

From this point shoulders will be worked separately. Place sts on side that does not have working yarn attached on holder.

First shoulder

***Row 1:** Work to neck edge.

Row 2: BO 2 sts at neck edge, work to end—6 sts.

Row 3: Work to neck edge.

Row 4: K2tog at neck edge, work to end—5 sts.

Rows 5–7: Work in St st.

Place rem 5 sts on holder.*

Second Shoulder

Join yarn at armhole edge. Work as first shoulder from * to *.

Back

Join yarn and work back and forth in St st until back is 1 row below last row of front sts, ending with WS row.

Next RS row: K5 sts, BO 10 sts, knit to end.

Turn garment inside out. Put shoulder sts back on needles and use 3-needle BO to join front and back shoulders tog.

Sleeves

Using crochet hook for pickup (page 12), PU 28 sts around armhole. Knit in rnd in St st for ½" or desired sleeve length.

Work 2 rnds in K1, P1 ribbing.

BO in patt. Fasten off. Weave in yarn tails.

Neckband

Using crochet hook, PU 34 sts (or close even number) around neck.

Work 3 rnds in K1, P1 ribbing.

BO in patt. Fasten off.

Weave in yarn tails.

PANTS

Using blue yarn, CO 48 sts. Distribute sts on 3 needles and join in rnd.

Work 4 rnds in K1, P1 ribbing.

Knit until piece measures 2" from CO.

Divide for Legs

Knit first 24 sts of next rnd. Place rem 24 sts on waste yarn.

First Leg

Distribute first 24 sts on 3 dpns. On third needle, CO an additional 4 sts. These 4 extra sts will be crotch of legs. Join sts in rnd and knit until leg measures 1" from leg divide or desired length.

Work 3 rnds in K1, P1 ribbing.

BO in patt. Fasten off.

Second Leg

Distribute 24 sts for second leg on 3 needles and knit them. At end of 24 sts, use crochet hook and working yarn to PU 4 sts from other leg, where 4 sts were CO at crotch of first leg. Knit this leg in the rnd in same manner as the other.

Weave in yarn tails.

> **High-Waist Pants**
> You may think that the pants don't fit the doll properly because the waist comes up high on the doll's chest. This is intentional so the pants stay on better. The shirt covers the waist, so no one will know!

SHOES

These instructions are same as foot of Basic Baby Suit. Top of shoe is a rolled edge.

With white yarn, CO 16 sts. Distribute sts on 3 needles and join in rnd. The intersection of needles 1 and 3 is heel; needle 2 holds toe sts.

Rnd 1: Knit.

Rnd 2: K1, M1, K3, M1, K4, M1, K4, M1, K3, M1, K1–21 sts.

Rnd 3: K1, M1, K9, M1, K1, M1, K9, M1, K1–25 sts.

Rnd 4: K11, M1, K3, M1, K11–27 sts.

Rnd 5: K11, M1, K5, M1, K11–29 sts.

Rnd 6: Knit.

Rnd 7: Knit.

Rnd 8: K11, ssk, K3, K2tog, K11–27 sts.

Rnd 9: K11, ssk, K1, K2tog, K11–25 sts.

Rnd 10: K11, sl 1-K2tog-psso, K11–23 sts.

Rnd 11: Knit.

Rnd 12: K1, ssk, K6, ssk, K1, K2tog, K6, K2tog, K1–19 sts.

Knit 1 more rnd.

Switch to black yarn and knit 3 rnds.

BO all sts.

Sew bottom of shoe closed. Using tapestry needle, thread length of embroidery floss or yarn through top of shoe to resemble shoelaces (see photo on page 74). Tie lace and trim threads. Rep to make second shoe. Find a miniature skate board and take off.

Useful Information

STANDARD YARN-WEIGHT SYSTEM						
Yarn-Weight Symbol and Category Names	Super Fine 1	Fine 2	Light 3	Medium 4	Bulky 5	Super Bulky 6
Types of Yarns in Category	Sock, Fingering, Baby	Sport, Baby	DK, Light Worsted	Worsted, Afghan, Aran	Chunky, Craft, Rug	Bulky, Roving
Knit Gauge Ranges in Stockinette Stitch to 4"	27 to 32 sts	23 to 26 sts	21 to 24 sts	16 to 20 sts	12 to 15 sts	6 to 11 sts
Recommended Needle in U.S. Size Range	1 to 3	3 to 5	5 to 7	7 to 9	9 to 11	11 and larger
Recommended Needle in Metric Size Range	2.25 to 3.25 mm	3.25 to 3.75 mm	3.75 to 4.5 mm	4.5 to 5.5 mm	5.5 to 8 mm	8 mm and larger

SKILL LEVELS

■□□□ **Beginner:** Projects for first-time knitters using basic knit and purl stitches; minimal shaping.

■■□□ **Easy:** Projects using basic stitches, repetitive stitch patterns, and simple color changes; simple shaping and finishing.

■■■□ **Intermediate:** Projects using a variety of stitches, such as basic cables and lace, simple intarsia, and techniques for double-pointed needles and knitting in the round; midlevel shaping.

■■■■ **Experienced:** Projects using advanced techniques and stitches, such as short rows, Fair Isle, more intricate intarsia, cables, lace patterns, and numerous color changes.

METRIC CONVERSIONS

Yards x .91 = meters

Meters x 1.09 = yards

Grams x .035 = ounces

Ounces x 28.35 = grams

Abbreviations and Glossary

approx	approximately
beg	begin(ning)
BO	bind off
CC	contrasting color
ch	chain
CO	cast on
cont	continue(ing)(s)
dec	decrease(ing)(s)
dpn(s)	double-pointed needle(s)
g	grams
garter st	garter stitch. **Back and forth:** knit every row. **In the round:** knit 1 round, purl 1 round.
inc	increase(ing)(s)
K	knit
K1f&b	knit into front and back of same stitch (1 stitch increased) (page 11)
K2tog	knit 2 stitches together (1 stitch decreased)
kw	knitwise
LH	left hand
M1	make 1 stitch (page 10)
MC	main color
m	meters
mm	millimeters
oz	ounces
P	purl
P2tog	purl 2 stitches together (1 stitch decreased)
patt	pattern
pm	place marker
psso	pass slipped stitch over
PU	pick up and knit
RH	right hand
rem	remaining
rep(s)	repeat(s)
rnd(s)	round(s)
RS	right side
sc	single crochet
sl	slip
sl 1-K2tog-psso	slip 1 stitch as if to knit, knit 2 stitches together, pass the slipped stitch over the 2 stitches knit together (2 stitches decreased)
sk2p	slip 1 stitch, knit 2 stitches together, pass slipped stitch over (2 stitches decreased)
ssk	slip 2 stitches knitwise, 1 at a time, to right needle, then insert left needle from left to right into front loops and knit 2 stitches together (1 stitch decreased)
st(s)	stitch(es)
St st	stockinette stitch. **Back and forth:** knit on right side, purl on wrong side. **In the round:** knit every round.
tbl	through back loop(s)
tog	together
WS	wrong side
yd(s)	yard(s)
YO	yarn over

Resources

Contact the following companies to find the materials used in this book.

YARNS

Bernat

www.bernat.com

Boa (100% polyester; 50 g/1.75 oz; 71 yds/65 m) 5

Crystal Palace Yarns

www.straw.com

Fizz (100% soft polyester; 50 g; 120 yds) 4

Splash (100% polyester; 100 g; 85 yds) 5

Dale of Norway

www.dale.no/us

Falk Dalegarn (100% washable wool; 50 g; 116 yds) 3

Frog Tree Yarns

www.frogtreeyarns.com

Alpaca Sport Melange (100% alpaca; 50 g/1.75 oz; 128 yds) 2

Alpaca Wool; Fingering Weight (100% alpaca; 50 g/1.75 oz; 215 yds) 1

Alpaca Wool; Sport Weight (100% alpaca; 50 g/1.75 oz; 130 yds) 3

Knit Picks

www.knitpicks.com

Crayon (100% pima cotton; 50 g; 128 yds) 3

Gloss DK (70% merino wool, 30% silk; 50 g; 123 yds) 3

Merino Style (100% merino wool; 50 g; 123 yds) 3

Palette (100% Peruvian highland wool; 50 g; 231 yds) 1

Simply Cotton Sport Weight (100% organic cotton; 50 g; 164 yds) 2

Swish DK (100% superwash merino wool; 50 g; 123 yds) 3

Lion Brand Yarn

www.lionbrandyarn.com

Fun Fur (100% polyester; 50 g/1.75 oz; 64 yds/58 m) 5

Wool-Ease (86% acrylic, 10% wool, 4% rayon; 85 g/3 oz; 197 yds/180 m) 4

Naturally Caron

www.naturallycaron.com

Spa (75% microdenier acrylic; 25% rayon from bamboo; 85 g/3 oz; 251 yds/230 m) 3

Noro

Distributed by Knitting Fever: www.knittingfever.com

Shirakaba (42% silk, 40% cotton, 18% wool; 50 g; 136 yds/125 m) 3

Patons

www.patonsyarns.com

Allure (100% nylon; 50 g/1.75 oz; 47 yds/43 m) 5

KNITTING NEEDLES

Brittany

www.brittanyneedles.com

Birch Double-Pointed Needles

Knit Picks

www.knitpicks.com

Harmony Double-Pointed Needles